Math
Grade 1

Printed in the U.S.A.

ISBN 978-0-544-26819-7

8 9 10 0928 22 21 20 19 18

4500702691 B C D E F G

Core Skills Math

GRADE 1

Table of Contents

Table of Contents
Core Skills Math, Grade 1

Mathematics Correlation Chart

Skills	Page Numbers
Addition	9, 10, 11, 12, 14, 15, 16, 28, 29, 30, 32, 33, 34, 35, 78, 79, 80, 81, 87, 125, 126, 127, 128, 129, 130, 132, 134, 135, 136, 137, 138, 145
Addition and Subtraction Equations	118, 119, 120, 121, 122
Addition and Subtraction Strategies	26, 44, 45, 77, 82, 85, 86, 124, 131, 133, 139, 140, 141, 142, 143
Counting	1, 2, 3, 4, 5, 6, 68, 69, 70, 71, 72, 73, 74, 75, 123
Fractions	100, 101, 102, 103, 104
Graphs and Charts	8, 94, 95, 96, 97, 98, 99
Length	90, 91, 92, 93
Money	113, 114, 115, 116, 117
Place Value	7, 59, 60, 61, 62, 63, 64, 65, 66, 67, 76
Problem Solving	13, 17, 22, 27, 31, 36, 37, 38, 42, 88, 89, 112, 144
Shapes	46, 47, 48, 49, 50, 51, 52, 53, 54, 55, 56, 57, 58
Subtraction	18, 19, 20, 21, 23, 24, 25, 39, 40, 41, 43, 83, 84
Time	105, 106, 107, 108, 109, 110, 111

One, Two, Three

Circle each pair.

Put a counter on each bird. Write how many.

1.

_____

- - - - - - - - - -

_____

2.

_____

- - - - - - - - - -

_____

3.

_____

- - - - - - - - - -

_____

NUMBER SENSE

4. Which shows 1 more than a pair? Circle the group.

Name _____ Date _____

Four and Five

Write how many.

1.

_____   _____   _____

- - - - - - - -   - - - - - - - -   - - - - - - - -

_____   _____   _____

2.

_____   _____   _____

- - - - - - - -   - - - - - - - -   - - - - - - - -

_____   _____   _____

3.

_____   _____   _____

- - - - - - - -   - - - - - - - -   - - - - - - - -

_____   _____   _____

NUMBER SENSE

4. Circle the group that has more than 3. Draw an X on the groups that have the same number.

2

Name _____ Date _____

Zero

Write 0.

Write how many .

1.

2.

3.

4.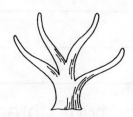

5.

6.

NUMBER SENSE

7. Circle the group that has more than 4. Draw an X on the groups that have the same number.

 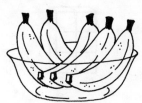 

3

Name _____ Date _____

Six and Seven

Write how many. Circle the number word.

1.

_____
------
six

five ⬭six⬭

2.

_____

_____

four five

3.

_____

_____

zero one

4.

_____

_____

five six

5.

_____

_____

six seven

6.

_____

_____

two three

VISUAL THINKING

7. Circle the groups that have more than 5. Draw an X on the groups that have fewer than 5.

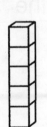 5

Eight and Nine

Which groups have 8? Circle them.

1.

  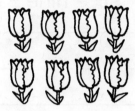

Which groups have 9? Circle them.

2.

NUMBER SENSE

3. Circle the group that has more.

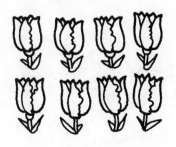 

5

Ten

Circle how many. Then write the number.

1.

six (nine) ten

_____

– – – 9 – – –

_____

2.

five six seven

_____

– – – – – – –

_____

3.

ten zero two

_____

– – – – – – –

_____

4.

eight three one

_____

– – – – – – –

_____

REASONING

5. Which group of dolphins has 2 fewer than 9?
Circle the group.

Name _____ Date _____

Comparing Numbers

Write how many. Then circle the number that is greater.

1.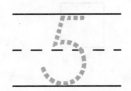

_____ _____

_6_  _5_

2.

_____ _____

_ _ _ _ _ _ _ _ _ _

Write how many. Then circle the number that is less.

3.

_____ _____

_ _ _ _ _ _ _ _ _ _

_____ _____

4.

_____ _____

_ _ _ _ _ _ _ _ _ _

_____ _____

REASONING

Complete the sentences. Use these words.   six   ten

_____

_ _ _ _ _ _ _ _ _

5. Ten is greater than _____.

_ _ _ _ _ _ _ _ _

6. Six is less than _____.

7

Problem Solving

MAKE A PICTOGRAPH

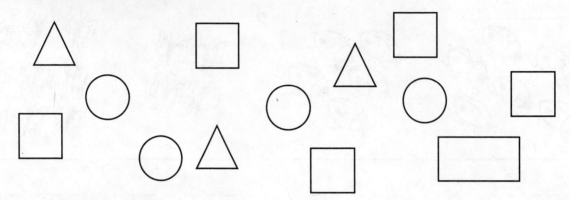

1. Count each shape.
Draw shapes to complete the graph.

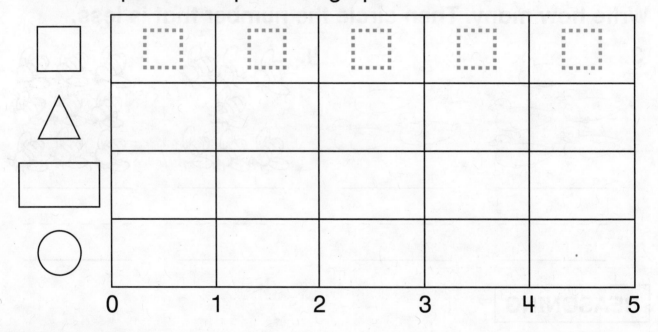

REASONING

Look at the graph.

2. Circle the one with more.

3. Circle the one with fewer.

Unit 1
Core Skills Math, Grade 1

Understanding Addition

Tell a story to a friend. Write how many.

How many?	How many join?	How many in all?

1.

   1 ___   1 ___   5 ___

2.

   ___   ___   ___

3.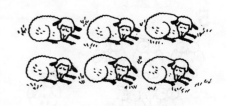

   ___   ___   ___

PROBLEM SOLVING

Make up a story. Write how many in all.

4.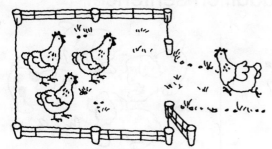

5.

___   ___

9

Name _____ Date _____

Addition Sentences

Write the addition sentences.

1.

2 + 1 = 3

2.

____ + ____ = ____

3.

____ + ____ = ____

4.

____ + ____ = ____

5.

____ + ____ = ____

6.

____ + ____ = ____

STORY CORNER

7. Tell a story to a friend. Write an addition sentence.

____ + ____ = ____

Order in Addition

Use counters. Draw X to show how many. Write the sum.

1.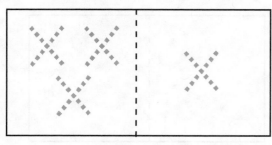

$$3 + 1 = \underline{4}$$

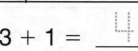

$$1 + 3 = \underline{4}$$

2.

$$2 + 4 = \underline{}$$

$$4 + 2 = \underline{}$$

3.

$$4 + 1 = \underline{}$$

$$1 + 4 = \underline{}$$

REASONING

4. Circle the pair that shows the same number.

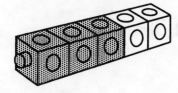 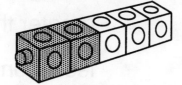 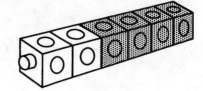

Adding Zero

Use counters. Draw dots to show how many. Write the sum.

1.

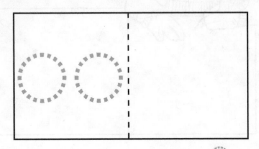

$2 + 0 =$ ____ 2

2.

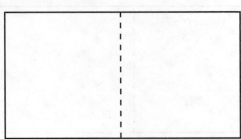

$0 + 3 =$ ____

3.

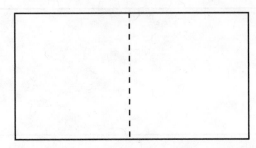

$0 + 5 =$ ____

4.

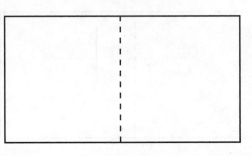

$1 + 0 =$ ____

5.

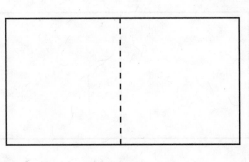

$6 + 0 =$ ____

6.

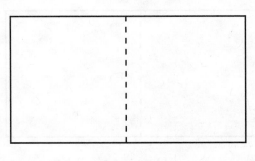

$0 + 4 =$ ____

NUMBER SENSE

7. Circle the better estimate.

$4 + 0 =$ ____ ?

greater than 5

less than 5

Name _____ Date _____

More Subtraction Sentences

Cross out. Then write how many are left.

1.

$4 - 2 =$ ___

2.

$6 - 1 =$ ___

3.

$5 - 2 =$ ___

4.

$4 - 1 =$ ___

5.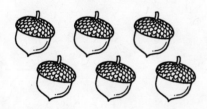

$6 - 2 =$ ___

6.

$5 - 0 =$ ___

STORY CORNER

7. Tell a story to a friend. Write the subtraction sentence.

___ $-$ ___ $=$ ___

Problem Solving

CHOOSE THE OPERATION

Tell a story to answer each question. Circle Add or Subtract.

1.

How many  are left?

Add   (Subtract)

2.

How many 🐴 in all?

Add   Subtract

Match each number sentence.

3.    •   • 6 − 0 = 6

4.    •   • 4 − 1 = 3

5.    •   • 4 + 1 = 5

6.    •   • 2 + 3 = 5

REASONING

7. Write the missing sign.

3 ◯ 3 = 6   3 ◯ 3 = 0   0 ◯ 3 = 3

22

Name _____ Date _____

Subtraction Combinations

Put in 4 ◯ .

```
┌─────────────────────────────────────────┐
│                                         │
│                                         │
│                                         │
│                                         │
│                                         │
└─────────────────────────────────────────┘
```

Find ways to subtract from 4.

1. $4 - 2 = 2$ **2.** $4 - \underline{\quad} = \underline{\quad}$

3. $4 - \underline{\quad} = \underline{\quad}$ **4.** $4 - \underline{\quad} = \underline{\quad}$

5. $4 - \underline{\quad} = \underline{\quad}$

Subtract.

6. $3 - 1 = \underline{\quad}$ $5 - 0 = \underline{\quad}$ $4 - 4 = \underline{\quad}$

7. $6 - 6 = \underline{\quad}$ $2 - 1 = \underline{\quad}$ $1 - 0 = \underline{\quad}$

8. $4 - 3 = \underline{\quad}$ $3 - 2 = \underline{\quad}$ $6 - 4 = \underline{\quad}$

9. $2 - 2 = \underline{\quad}$ $5 - 2 = \underline{\quad}$ $6 - 1 = \underline{\quad}$

10. $3 - 0 = \underline{\quad}$ $6 - 3 = \underline{\quad}$ $1 - 1 = \underline{\quad}$

NUMBER SENSE

Circle the better estimate.

11. $9 - 3 = \underline{\ ?\ }$ more than 9   less than 9

23

Name _____   Date _____

More Subtraction Combinations

Put in 5

```
┌─────────────────────────────────────────────┐
│                                             │
│                                             │
│                                             │
│                                             │
└─────────────────────────────────────────────┘
```

Fir___ ___ys to subtract from 5.

___ – 5 = 0   **2.** 5 – ____ = ____

___ – ____ = ____   **4.** 5 – ____ = ____

5 – ____ = ____   **6.** 5 – ____ = ____

___ok for a pattern. Subtract.

7. 6 – 3 = ____   6 – 2 = ____   6 – 1 = ____

8. 5 – 2 = ____   5 – 1 = ____   5 – 0 = ____

9. 5 – 1 = ____   5 – 2 = ____   5 – 3 = ____

10. 4 – 0 = ____   4 – 1 = ____   4 – 2 = ____

NUMBER SENSE

11. Which answer will be the least?
Circle it. Then solve to check.

10 – 3 = ____   10 – 2 = ____   10 – 1 = ____

Unit 3
Core Skills Math, Grade 1

Name _____ Date _____

Vertical Subtraction

Subtract.

1.
$$\begin{array}{r} 4 \\ -\ 2 \\ \hline 2 \end{array}$$

2.
$$\begin{array}{r} 5 \\ -\ 1 \\ \hline \end{array}$$

3.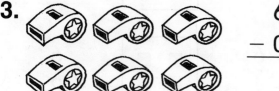
$$\begin{array}{r} 6 \\ -\ 0 \\ \hline \end{array}$$

4.
$$\begin{array}{r} 4 \\ -\ 3 \\ \hline \end{array}$$

5.
$$\begin{array}{r} 5¢ \\ -\ 5¢ \\ \hline ¢ \end{array}$$

6.
$$\begin{array}{r} 6¢ \\ -\ 1¢ \\ \hline ¢ \end{array}$$

7.
$$\begin{array}{r} 6¢ \\ -\ 4¢ \\ \hline ¢ \end{array}$$

8.
$$\begin{array}{r} 5¢ \\ -\ 4¢ \\ \hline ¢ \end{array}$$

VISUAL THINKING

9. Draw dots to continue the pattern.

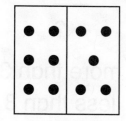 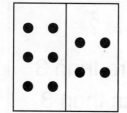 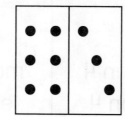 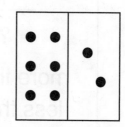 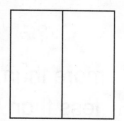

Unit 3
Core Skills Math, Grade 1

Addition and Subtraction

Add or subtract.

1. 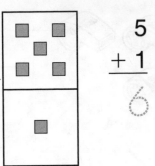 $\begin{array}{r} 5 \\ + 1 \\ \hline \end{array}$ 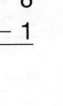 $\begin{array}{r} 6 \\ - 1 \\ \hline \end{array}$ $\begin{array}{r} 6 \\ - 5 \\ \hline \end{array}$

2. 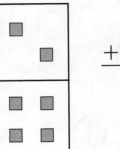 $\begin{array}{r} 2 \\ + 4 \\ \hline \end{array}$ $\begin{array}{r} 6 \\ - 4 \\ \hline \end{array}$ $\begin{array}{r} 6 \\ - 2 \\ \hline \end{array}$

3. 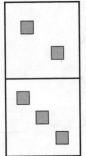 $\begin{array}{r} 2 \\ + 3 \\ \hline \end{array}$ $\begin{array}{r} 5 \\ - 3 \\ \hline \end{array}$ $\begin{array}{r} 5 \\ - 2 \\ \hline \end{array}$

NUMBER SENSE

4. Circle the better estimate.

$\begin{array}{r} 4 \\ + 1 \\ \hline ? \end{array}$	$\begin{array}{r} 4 \\ - 1 \\ \hline ? \end{array}$	$\begin{array}{r} 3 \\ + 2 \\ \hline ? \end{array}$	$\begin{array}{r} 3 \\ - 2 \\ \hline ? \end{array}$
more than 4 less than 4	more than 4 less than 4	more than 3 less than 3	more than 3 less than 3

Unit 3
Core Skills Math, Grade 1

Name _____ Date _____

Problem Solving

| CHOOSE THE QUESTION |

Circle the correct question.

1. Rosa sees 3 .
Then all of them fly away.

How many in all?

How many are left?

2. Chad counts 5 .
Then he sees 1 more.

How many in all?

How many are left?

3. Mrs. Davis finds 2 .
Then she finds 2 more.

How many in all?

How many are left?

4. Mr. Davis sees 2 .
Then 1 hops away.

How many in all?

How many are left?

5. Chad watches 4 .
Then 3 run away.

How many in all?

How many are left?

6. Rosa counts 3 .
Then she counts 3 more.

How many in all?

How many are left?

| STORY CORNER |

7. Tell a story about the picture.
Write the number sentence.

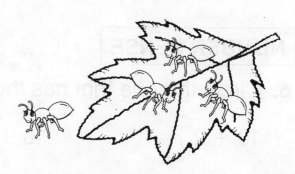

Unit 3
Core Skills Math, Grade 1

Counting On with Models

Count on to add. Write each sum.

1.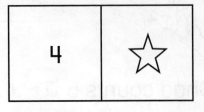

4 + 1 = _5_   4 + 2 = ____

2.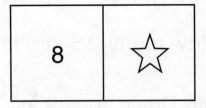

8 + 1 = ____   5 + 2 = ____

3.

5 + 1 = ____   2 + 2 = ____

4. 6 + 1 = ____   7 + 1 = ____   8 + 1 = ____

5. 8 + 2 = ____   7 + 2 = ____   6 + 2 = ____

NUMBER SENSE

6. Circle the one that has the greatest sum.

10 + 2   10 + 1   10 + 0

Unit 4
Core Skills Math, Grade 1

More Counting On

Count on to add. Write each sum.

1.
           $\begin{array}{r} 3 \\ +2 \\ \hline \end{array}$
           $\begin{array}{r} 5 \\ +2 \\ \hline \end{array}$
           $\begin{array}{r} 1 \\ +2 \\ \hline \end{array}$
           $\begin{array}{r} 8 \\ +2 \\ \hline \end{array}$

2. $\begin{array}{r} 2 \\ +1 \\ \hline \end{array}$
     $\begin{array}{r} 5 \\ +1 \\ \hline \end{array}$
     $\begin{array}{r} 8 \\ +1 \\ \hline \end{array}$
     $\begin{array}{r} 1 \\ +1 \\ \hline \end{array}$
     $\begin{array}{r} 9 \\ +1 \\ \hline \end{array}$
     $\begin{array}{r} 7 \\ +1 \\ \hline \end{array}$

3. $\begin{array}{r} 3 \\ +3 \\ \hline \end{array}$
     $\begin{array}{r} 7 \\ +3 \\ \hline \end{array}$
     $\begin{array}{r} 5 \\ +3 \\ \hline \end{array}$
     $\begin{array}{r} 1 \\ +3 \\ \hline \end{array}$
     $\begin{array}{r} 4 \\ +3 \\ \hline \end{array}$
     $\begin{array}{r} 6 \\ +3 \\ \hline \end{array}$

4. $\begin{array}{r} 7 \\ +2 \\ \hline \end{array}$
     $\begin{array}{r} 5 \\ +3 \\ \hline \end{array}$
     $\begin{array}{r} 9 \\ +1 \\ \hline \end{array}$
     $\begin{array}{r} 8 \\ +2 \\ \hline \end{array}$
     $\begin{array}{r} 6 \\ +3 \\ \hline \end{array}$
     $\begin{array}{r} 6 \\ +2 \\ \hline \end{array}$

5. $\begin{array}{r} 4 \\ +3 \\ \hline \end{array}$
     $\begin{array}{r} 4 \\ +2 \\ \hline \end{array}$
     $\begin{array}{r} 8 \\ +1 \\ \hline \end{array}$
     $\begin{array}{r} 7 \\ +3 \\ \hline \end{array}$
     $\begin{array}{r} 5 \\ +2 \\ \hline \end{array}$
     $\begin{array}{r} 5 \\ +1 \\ \hline \end{array}$

NUMBER SENSE

6. Circle the one that has the least sum.

    $9 + 2$ $9 + 1$ $9 + 3$

Counting On 1, 2, and 3

Count on to add. Write each sum.

1.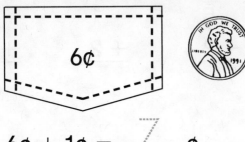

6¢ + 1¢ = _____ ¢

2.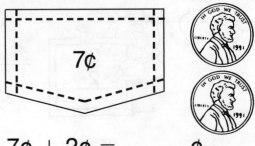

7¢ + 2¢ = _____ ¢

3.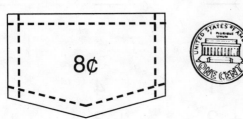

8¢ + 1¢ = _____ ¢

4.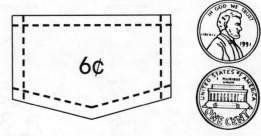

6¢ + 2¢ = _____ ¢

5.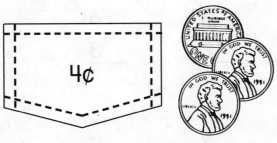

4¢ + 3¢ = _____ ¢

6.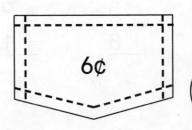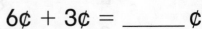

6¢ + 3¢ = _____ ¢

REASONING

Solve.

7. Lee has 5¢.

Kara has 3¢ more than Lee.

Tom has 2¢ more than Kara.

How much money does Tom have? _____ ¢

Unit 4
Core Skills Math, Grade 1

Problem Solving

MAKE A MODEL

Use counters. Then write the number sentence.

1. Sal saw 3 shows at the fair. Then he saw 2 more. How many shows did he see?

   _3_ $\oplus$ _2_ = _5_

   _5_ shows

2. Donna won 5 prizes. Then she won 2 more. How many prizes did she win?

   _____ ◯ _____ = _____

   _____ prizes

3. Sue had 6 tickets for rides. Hector had 3 tickets. How many tickets did they have?

   _____ ◯ _____ = _____

   _____ tickets

4. Hector rode 4 slow rides. Then he rode 3 fast rides. How many rides did he go on?

   _____ ◯ _____ = _____

   _____ rides

STORY CORNER

5. Look at the picture. Make up a story problem.

37

Problem Solving

TOO MUCH INFORMATION: ADDITION

Draw a line through the sentence you do not need. Then solve.

1. There are 4 cars on the road.
   ~~There are 2 trucks on the road.~~
   Then 3 more cars come.
   How many cars are there?

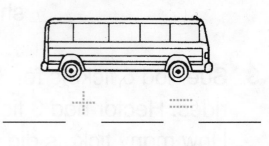

   _4_ + _3_ = _7_

   __7__ cars

2. Mr. Ladd sees 4 buses.
   Then he sees 4 more buses.
   He sees 1 train, too.
   How many buses does he see?

   ___ + ___ = ___

   _____ buses

3. Anna counts 5 trees.
   She counts 3 stop signs.
   Then she counts 6 more
   stop signs. How many stop
   signs does she see?

   ___ + ___ = ___

   _____ stop signs

STORY CORNER

4. Look at the picture. Make up a
   story problem. Tell it to a friend.
   Have a friend solve it.

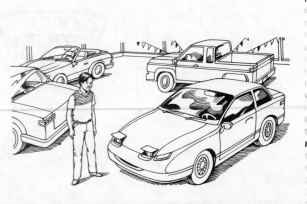

Name _____ Date _____

Count Back Using a Number Line

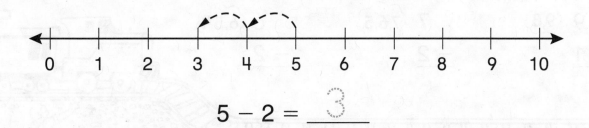

$5 - 2 = \underline{}$

Use the number line. Count back to subtract.

4, 3

1. $4 - 1 = \underline{}$

2. $6 - 1 = \underline{}$

3. $5 - 1 = \underline{}$

4. $9 - 2 = \underline{}$

5. $7 - 1 = \underline{}$

3, 2

$3 - 1 = \underline{}$

$5 - 2 = \underline{}$

$7 - 2 = \underline{}$

$3 - 2 = \underline{}$

$9 - 1 = \underline{}$

6, 5, 4

$6 - 2 = \underline{}$

$8 - 1 = \underline{}$

$4 - 2 = \underline{}$

$10 - 1 = \underline{}$

$10 - 2 = \underline{}$

NUMBER SENSE

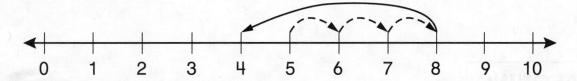

Use the number line. Write the number.

6. Start at 5. Count on 3.
   Count back 4.
   What is the number? _____

7. Start at 6. Count on 4.
   Count back 4.
   What is the number? _____

Unit 5
Core Skills Math, Grade 1

Name _____   Date _____

Count Back to Subtract

9 (9,8)   7 (7,6,5)   6 (6,5,4)
− 1   − 2   − 2
8   5   4

Count back to subtract.

1.   8   10   4   5   3   6
        − 1   − 1   − 1   − 1   − 1   − 1

2.   3   10   5   4   9   8
        − 2   − 2   − 2   − 2   − 2   − 2

3.   7   9   9   6   5   7
        − 1   − 2   − 1   − 2   − 1   − 2

| REASONING |

Solve.

4. Mario is 5 years old. Sam is 2 years
   younger than Mario. Fumi is 1 year
   younger than Sam. How old is Fumi?

_____ years old

Counting Back 1, 2, and 3

Count back to subtract. Use your answers from the box to color the picture blue.

1.

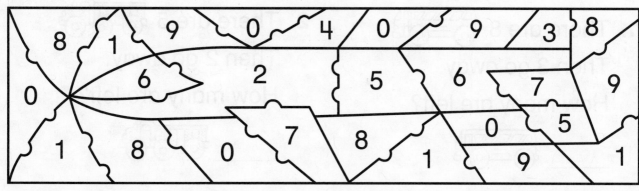

$4 - 2 = \underline{2}$ $8 - 1 = \underline{\hspace{1cm}}$ $9 - 3 = \underline{\hspace{1cm}}$

$8 - 3 = \underline{\hspace{1cm}}$ $9 - 2 = \underline{\hspace{1cm}}$ $7 - 1 = \underline{\hspace{1cm}}$

$5 - 1 = \underline{\hspace{1cm}}$ $6 - 3 = \underline{\hspace{1cm}}$ $7 - 2 = \underline{\hspace{1cm}}$

2.

8	5	3	6	9	7
− 2	− 3	− 1	− 2	− 1	− 3

NUMBER SENSE

Look at each pair. Circle the fact that has the answer that is less. Solve to check.

3. 7   7   **4.** 8   8   **5.** 9   9
    − 1   − 3   − 1   − 2   − 2   − 3

Unit 5
Core Skills Math, Grade 1

Name _____ Date _____

Problem Solving

MAKE A MODEL

Use counters to solve.

1. There are 8 .

   Then 3 go away.

   How many are left?

   _5_

2. There are 5 .

   Then 2 go away.

   How many are left?

   _____

3. There are 7 🚗.

   Then 2 go away.

   How many are left?

   _____

4. There are 8 🚲.

   Then 2 go away.

   How many are left?

   _____

5. There are 6 🚌.

   There are 3 🚚.

   How many more 🚌

   than 🚚 ?

   _____ more

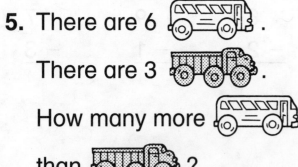

6. There are 9 🚐.

   There are 3 🚗.

   How many more 🚐

   than 🚗 ?

   _____ more

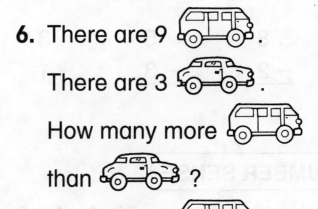

STORY CORNER

7. Make up two story problems about a 🚌.
   Tell them to a friend. Have your friend solve each one.

Unit 5
Core Skills Math, Grade 1

Name _____ Date _____

Subtracting Zero and Related Facts

Subtract. Write each difference.

1. $\begin{array}{r} 6 \\ -1 \\ \hline \end{array}$ $\begin{array}{r} 6 \\ -5 \\ \hline \end{array}$ $\begin{array}{r} 3 \\ -0 \\ \hline \end{array}$ $\begin{array}{r} 3 \\ -3 \\ \hline \end{array}$ $\begin{array}{r} 8 \\ -3 \\ \hline \end{array}$ $\begin{array}{r} 8 \\ -5 \\ \hline \end{array}$

2. $\begin{array}{r} 9 \\ -2 \\ \hline \end{array}$ $\begin{array}{r} 9 \\ -7 \\ \hline \end{array}$ $\begin{array}{r} 4 \\ -1 \\ \hline \end{array}$ $\begin{array}{r} 4 \\ -3 \\ \hline \end{array}$ $\begin{array}{r} 10 \\ -3 \\ \hline \end{array}$ $\begin{array}{r} 10 \\ -7 \\ \hline \end{array}$

3. $\begin{array}{r} 10 \\ -2 \\ \hline \end{array}$ $\begin{array}{r} 10 \\ -8 \\ \hline \end{array}$ $\begin{array}{r} 7 \\ -2 \\ \hline \end{array}$ $\begin{array}{r} 7 \\ -5 \\ \hline \end{array}$ $\begin{array}{r} 9 \\ -3 \\ \hline \end{array}$ $\begin{array}{r} 9 \\ -6 \\ \hline \end{array}$

4. $\begin{array}{r} 7 \\ -3 \\ \hline \end{array}$ $\begin{array}{r} 7 \\ -4 \\ \hline \end{array}$ $\begin{array}{r} 5 \\ -3 \\ \hline \end{array}$ $\begin{array}{r} 5 \\ -2 \\ \hline \end{array}$ $\begin{array}{r} 10 \\ -1 \\ \hline \end{array}$ $\begin{array}{r} 10 \\ -9 \\ \hline \end{array}$

REASONING

Which boy is Terry? Circle him.

5. Jack has 3 balls.
Fred has 3 more balls
than Jack. Terry has
more balls than
Jack or Fred.

Unit 5
Core Skills Math, Grade 1

Addition and Subtraction

Write an addition fact. Cross out the black counters.
Then write the subtraction fact.

1.

$$5$$
$$+\ 1$$
$$\overline{6}$$

$$6$$
$$-\ 1$$
$$\overline{5}$$

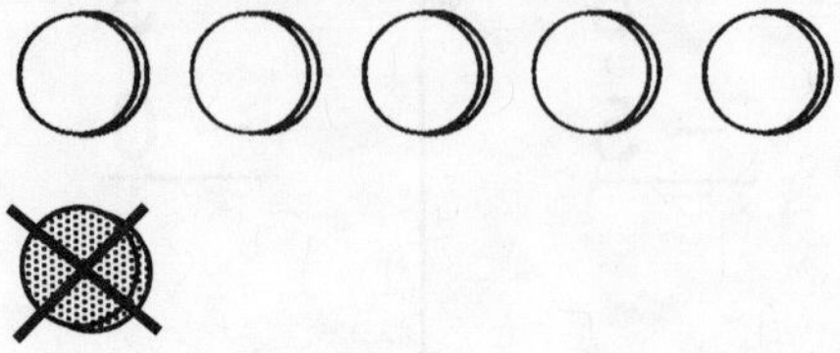

2.

$$+$$
$$\overline{}$$

$$-$$
$$\overline{}$$

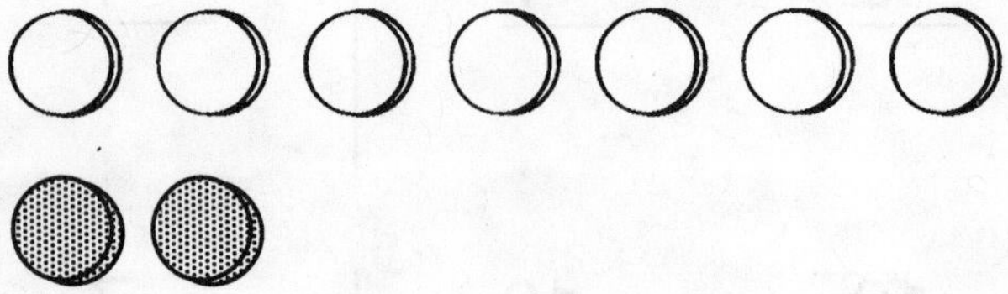

3.

$$+$$
$$\overline{}$$

$$-$$
$$\overline{}$$

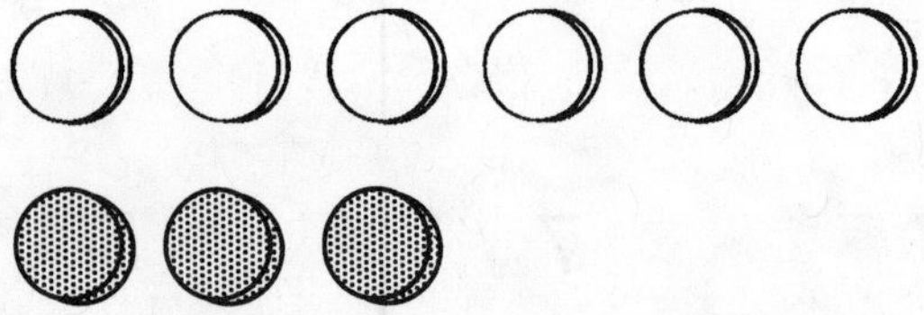

4.

$$+$$
$$\overline{}$$

$$-$$
$$\overline{}$$

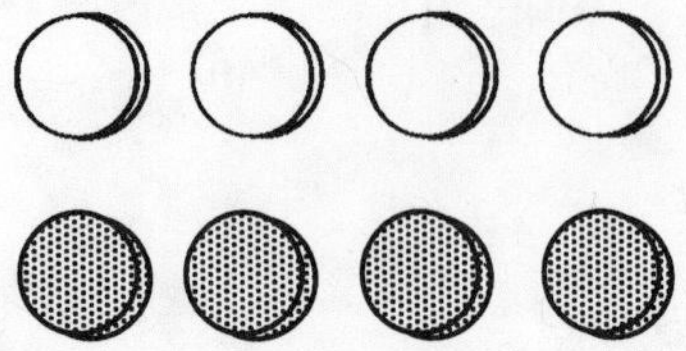

VISUAL THINKING

5. Think about the picture.
   Circle **Add** or **Subtract.**

Add   Subtract

Core Skills Math, Grade 1

Fact Families

Use cubes. Add or subtract.
Write the numbers in each fact family.

1. 5 + 1 = _6_   3 + 1 = ____   2 + 3 = ____

   1 + 5 = _6_   1 + 3 = ____   3 + 2 = ____

   6 − 1 = _5_   4 − 1 = ____   5 − 3 = ____

   6 − 5 = _1_   4 − 3 = ____   5 − 2 = ____

   _5_ , _1_ , _6_   ____ , ____ , ____   ____ , ____ , ____

Add or subtract.
Which sentence does not belong? Circle it.

2. 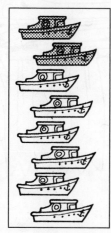   2 + 6 = ____

   6 + 2 = ____

   8 − 2 = ____

   7 − 2 = ____

   8 − 6 = ____

3. 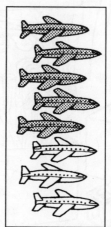   5 + 3 = ____

   3 + 5 = ____

   4 + 3 = ____

   8 − 5 = ____

   8 − 3 = ____

PROBLEM SOLVING

Write the numbers.

4. Our sum is 5. Our difference is 1.   ____ and ____

Identify Solid Shapes

cube   cone   sphere   cylinder   box

1. Color each cube shape red.
2. Color each sphere shape blue.
3. Circle each cylinder shape.
4. Draw an X on each cone shape.
5. Draw a line under each box shape.

STORY CORNER

6. Read this riddle. Circle the name of the shape.

I am a solid shape.
All my sides are flat.

cone   cube   sphere

Attributes of Solid Shapes

Use solid shapes. Circle each shape that will stack.

1.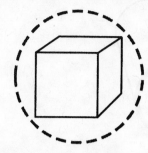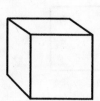

Draw an X on each shape that will roll.

2.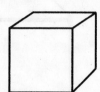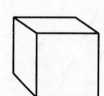

Color each shape that will slide.

3.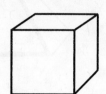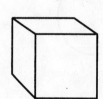

REASONING

Use solid shapes to build.
Circle the shape that must be on top. Tell why.

4.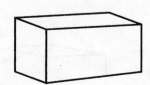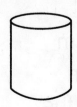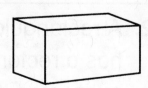

Unit 6
Core Skills Math, Grade 1

Name _____ Date _____

Solid and Plane Shapes

Match the plane shape to the solid.

1.

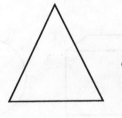
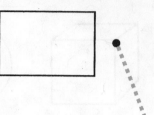
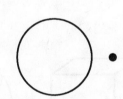

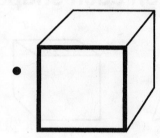
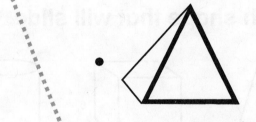
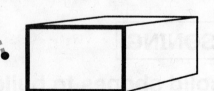

VISUAL THINKING

2. A rectangular prism
   has a rectangle on
   every side. Circle the
   rectangular prism.

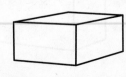

48

Name _____ Date _____

3-Dimensional Shapes

Use 3-dimensional shapes. Write the number of flat surfaces for each shape.

1. A cylinder has __2__ flat surfaces.

2. A rectangular prism has _____ flat surfaces.

3. A cone has _____ flat surface.

4. A cube has _____ flat surfaces.

5. A sphere has _____ flat surfaces.

| PROBLEM SOLVING |

Circle the object that matches the clue.

6. Mike finds an object that can slide and roll.

Name _____ Date _____

Open and Closed Figures

Color inside each closed figure.
Circle the figures that are open.

open   closed

1.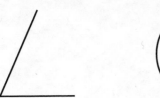

2.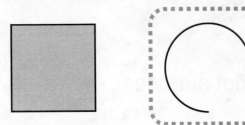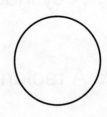

Color inside each rectangle.
3.

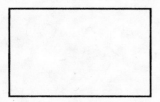 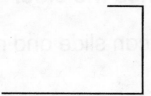  

VISUAL THINKING

4. Circle the letters that are open figures.

C D G N O S

Name _____ Date _____

Sides and Corners

Trace each side 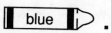.

Draw a 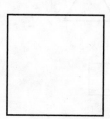 on each corner.

Write how many sides and corners.

1. corner

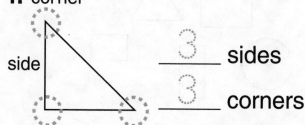

side

___3___ sides

___3___ corners

2.

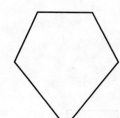

_____ sides

_____ corners

3.

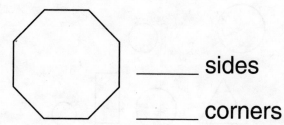

_____ sides

_____ corners

4.

_____ sides

_____ corners

5.

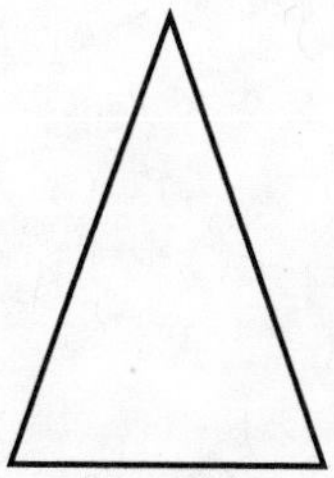

_____ sides

_____ corners

6.

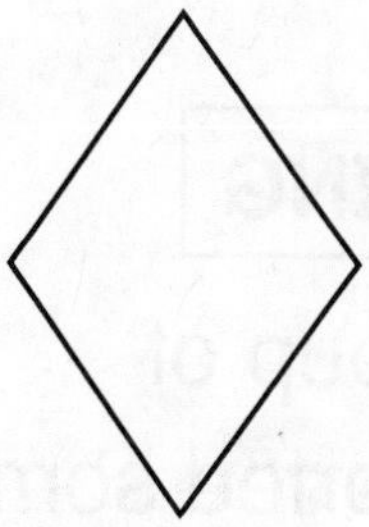

_____ sides

_____ corners

REASONING

7. What kind of figure
has 2 sides and 1 corner?
Circle the answer.

open figure   closed figure

51

Sort 2-Dimensional Shapes

Read the sorting rule. Circle the shapes that follow the rule.

1. not curved

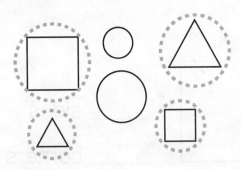

2. 4 corners

3. more than 3 sides

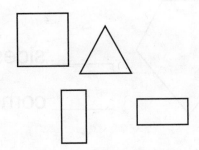

4. curved

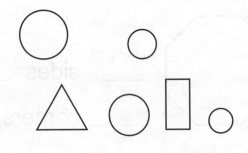

PROBLEM SOLVING

5. Katie had a group of objects. She sorted some shapes into the smaller group shown. Write a sorting rule to tell how Katie sorted.

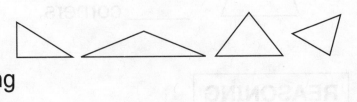

_____

_____

_____

Name ______________________ Date ____________

Combine 3-Dimensional Shapes

Use 3-dimensional shapes.

Combine.	**Which new shape can you make? Circle it.**	
1. 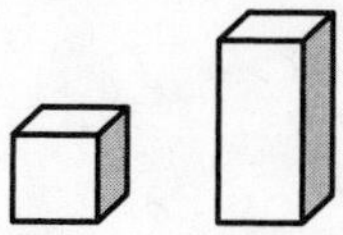	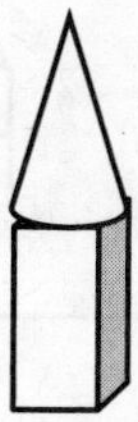	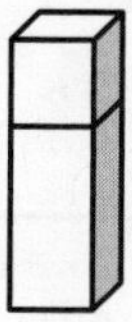
2. 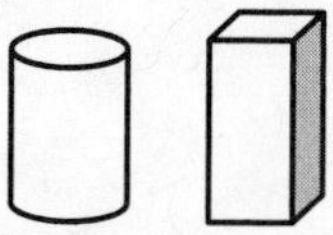	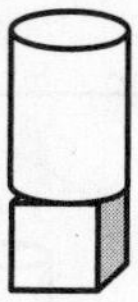	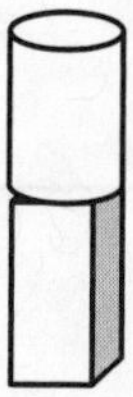
3. 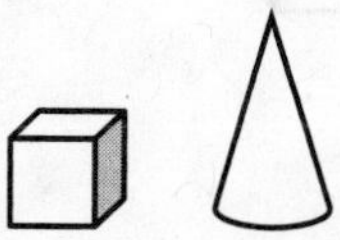	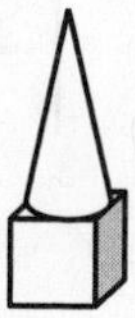	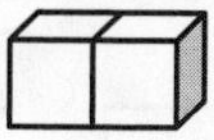

PROBLEM SOLVING

4. Circle the shapes you could use to model the bird feeder.

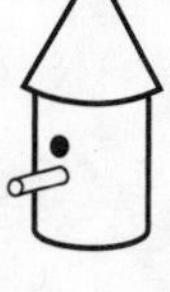

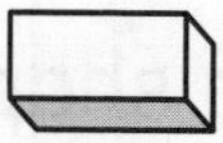

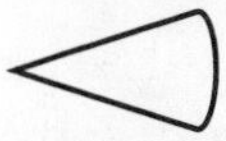

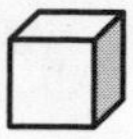

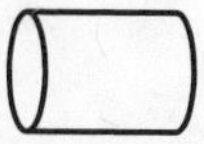

Make New 3-Dimensional Shapes

Use 3-dimensional shapes.

Build and Repeat.	**Combine. Which new shape can you make? Circle it.**
1. 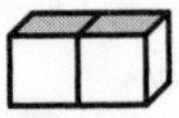	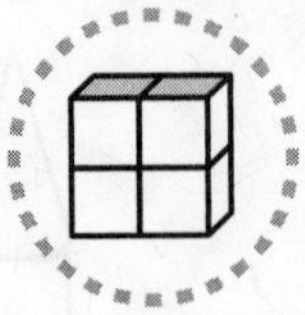 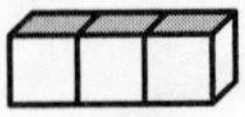
2. 	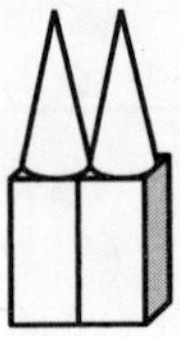 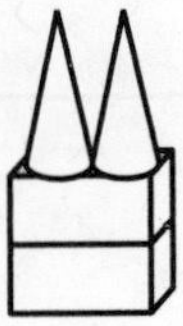
3. 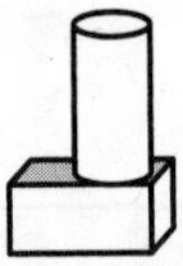	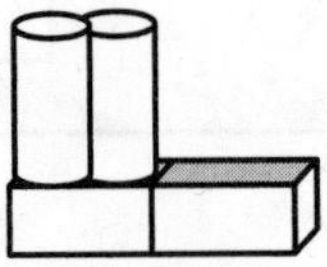 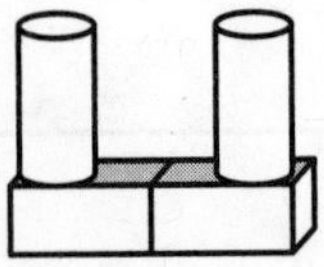

PROBLEM SOLVING

4. Dave builds this shape.
Then he repeats and combines.
Draw a shape he can make.

Making Solid Shapes

Use cubes. Make the shape. Tell how many cubes you used.

1.

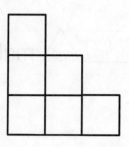

_____ cubes

2.

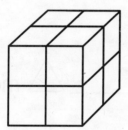

_____ cubes

3.

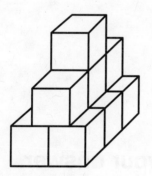

_____ cubes

VISUAL THINKING

4. Circle the shapes that have a round bottom or a round top.

cone   cube   cylinder

5. Circle the shapes that have corners.

cube   rectangular prism   sphere

Combine 2-Dimensional Shapes

Use pattern blocks. Draw to show the blocks.
Write how many blocks you used.

1. How many △ make a ⬡? _____ △ make a ⬡.

2. How many △ make a ◇? _____ △ make a ◇.

PROBLEM SOLVING

Use pattern blocks. Draw to show your answer.

3. 2 ⬡ make a ⬡.

How many ⬡ make 4 ⬡?

_____ ⬡ make 4 ⬡.

Combine More Shapes

**Circle two shapes that can combine
to make the shape on the left.**

1.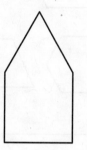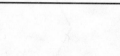

2.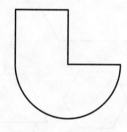

3.

PROBLEM SOLVING

4. Draw lines to show how the shapes
on the left combine to make the new shape.

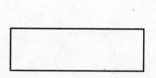   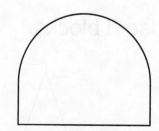

Find Shapes in Shapes

Use two pattern blocks to make the shape.
Draw a line to show your model. Circle the blocks you use.

1.

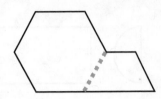

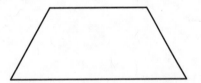

2.

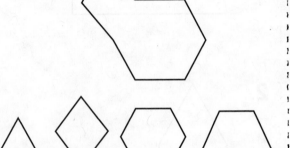

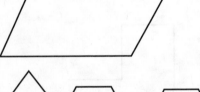

3.

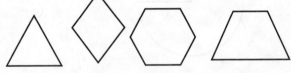

4.

PROBLEM SOLVING

Make the shape to the right. Use the
number of pattern blocks listed.
Write how many of each block you use.

5. Use 3 blocks.

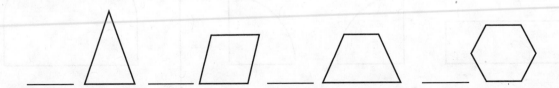

Groups of 10

Circle groups of 10. Write how many groups you made. Write how many in all.

1.

_____3_____ groups of 10

_____30_____ in all

2.

_____ groups of 10

_____

3.

_____ groups of 10

_____

NUMBER SENSE

4. Which group has the greater number? Circle it.

4 groups of 10   2 groups of 10

59

Grouping Tens

Complete the table.

		How many tens?	How many in all?
1.	♥ ♥ ♥ ♥ ♥ ♥ ♥ ♥ ♥ ♥	1 ten	10 stickers in all
2.	♥ ♥ ♥ ♥ ♥ ♥ ♥ ♥ ♥ ♥ ♥ ♥ ♥ ♥ ♥ ♥ ♥ ♥ ♥ ♥	_____ tens	_____ stickers in all
3.	(4 rows of hearts)	_____ tens	_____ stickers in all
4.	(5 rows of hearts)	_____ tens	_____ stickers in all
5.	(6 rows of hearts)	_____ tens	_____ stickers in all
6.	(8 rows of hearts)	_____ tens	_____ stickers in all

NUMBER SENSE

Which is the greater number? Circle it.

7. 30   7 tens   **8.** 4 tens   50

60

Tens and Ones to 20

Write how many.

1. 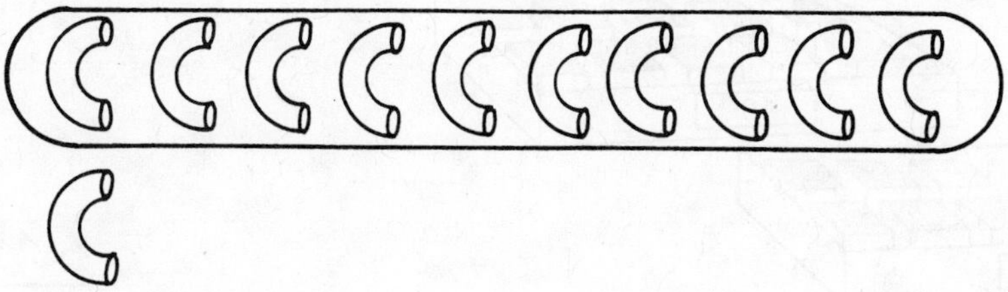 CCCCCCCCCC
   C

_____ ten _____ one

2. 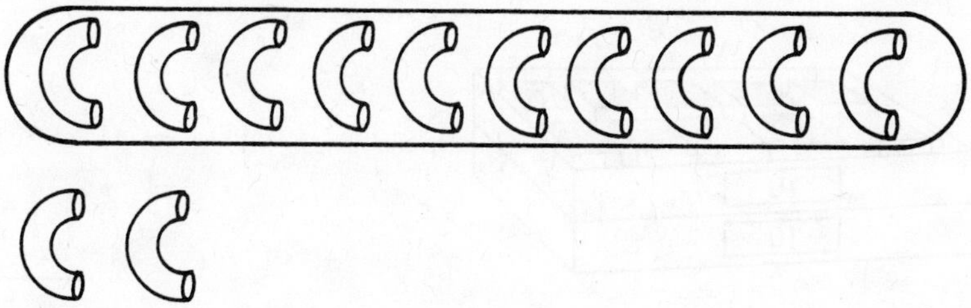 CCCCCCCCCC
   C C

_____ ten _____ ones

_____

3. 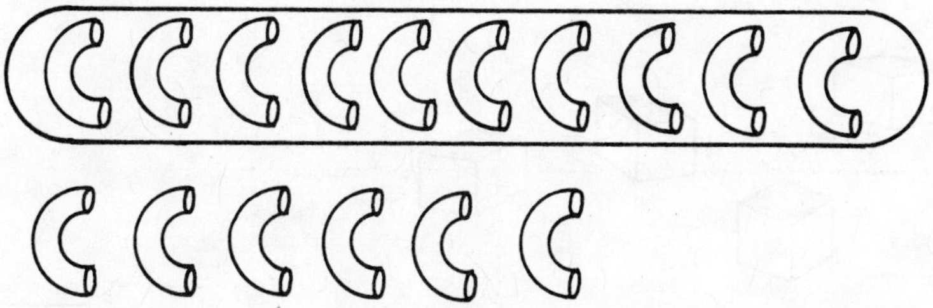 CCCCCCCCCC
   C C C C C C

_____ ten _____ ones

_____

4. 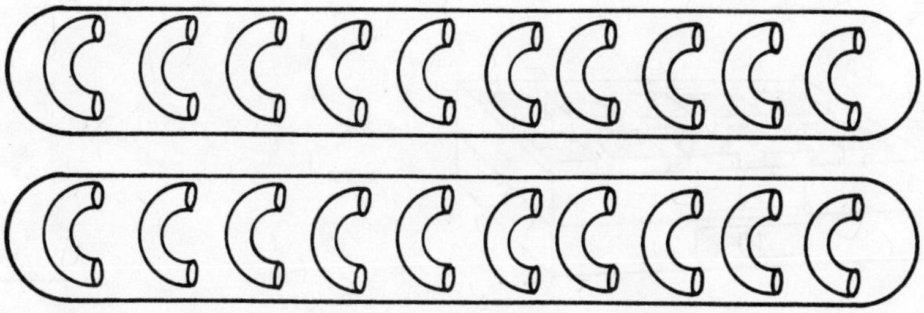 CCCCCCCCCC
   CCCCCCCCCC

_____ tens _____ ones

_____

NUMBER SENSE

5. How many [red ⟩ are there?
   Circle the better estimate.

   more than 10   fewer than 10

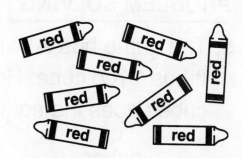

Name _____ Date _____

Tens and Ones to 50

Count. Write how many in all.

1.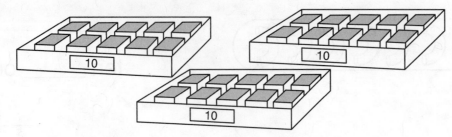

30

2.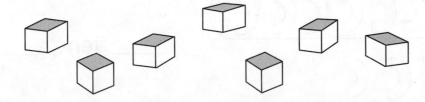

_____

3.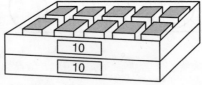

_____

4.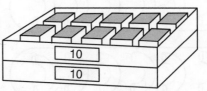

_____

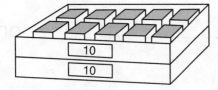

PROBLEM SOLVING

5. The game has 20 white cubes.
It has 1 red cube. How many
cubes does the game have in all?

_____ cubes

62

Unit 7
Core Skills Math, Grade 1

Name _____ Date _____

Tens and Ones to 80

Use place-value models. Complete the table.

1.

Tens	Ones	In All
6	5	65
3	6	____
5	4	____

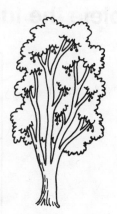

Count. Write how many in all.

2.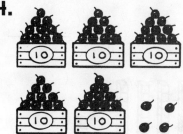

36

3.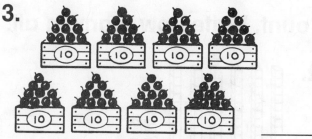

____

4.

____

5.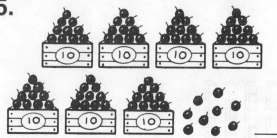

____

NUMBER SENSE

6. Circle the group that has the greater number.

   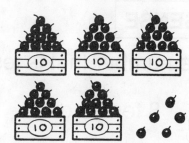

Unit 7
Core Skills Math, Grade 1

Tens and Ones to 100

Use place-value models.
Complete the table.

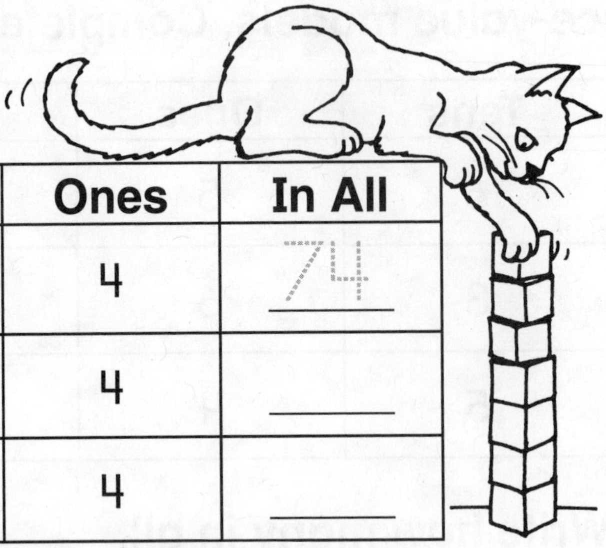

1.

Tens	Ones	In All
7	4	74
8	4	____
9	4	____

Count. Write how many in all.

2.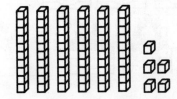

65

3.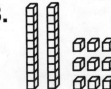

____

4.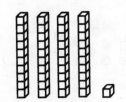

____

5.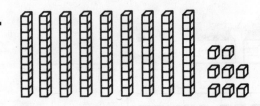

____

NUMBER SENSE

6. Circle the number that is less.

8 tens 6 ones   7 tens 6 ones

Unit 7
Core Skills Math, Grade 1

Name _____ Date _____

Comparing Numbers

Use place-value models.

Circle the number that is greater. Use **.**

1. (55)

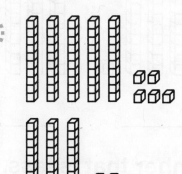

34

2. 46

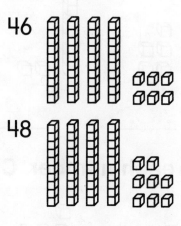

48

3. 28

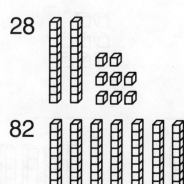

82

4. 69

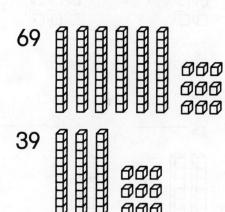

39

NUMBER SENSE

5. Which numbers are less than 50? Circle them in ▐ red ▷ .

| 34 | 78 | 12 | 99 | | 41 | 56 | 29 | 21 |

50

| 73 | 22 | 44 | 20 | | 38 | 63 | 92 | 85 |

Unit 7
Core Skills Math, Grade 1

Comparing Numbers Given a Model

Write each number. Then circle the greater number.

1.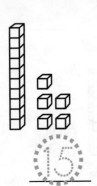

   15   12

2.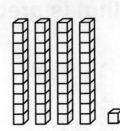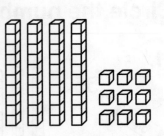

   _____   _____

Write each number. Circle the number that is less.

3.

   _____   _____

4.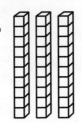

   _____   _____

5.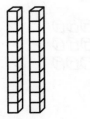

   _____   _____

6.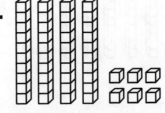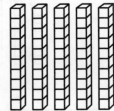

   _____   _____

PROBLEM SOLVING

Write the number.

7. I am 3 greater than 72.
   I am 1 less than 76.

   _____

8. I am 5 greater than 61.
   I am 3 less than 69.

   _____

Greater Than and Less Than

Use place-value models to show each pair of numbers. Then write < or > in each circle.

1. 56 ◯ 54   36 ◯ 37   7 ◯ 4

2. 57 ◯ 45   24 ◯ 21   48 ◯ 60

3. 12 ◯ 14   8 ◯ 11   35 ◯ 52

Write your own number sentences.

4. _____ > 64   _____ < 33   17 < _____

5. 29 ◯ _____   _____ ◯ 48   30 ◯ _____

REASONING

6. Circle the one that is greater.

   a number that comes before 75

   a number that comes after 75

Before, After, Between

Use place-value models. Write the numbers.

1.

before	between	after
21	22	23
_____	47	_____
_____	97	_____

Write the number that comes between.

2.

37 __38__ 39	12 _____ 14	20 _____ 22
91 _____ 93	25 _____ 27	78 _____ 80
22 _____ 24	86 _____ 88	32 _____ 34
61 _____ 63	44 _____ 46	80 _____ 82

REASONING

Circle Yes or No.

3. Does 56 come before 57?

Yes   No

4. Is 56 less than 57?

Yes   No

Number Patterns

Complete the table. Write the missing numbers.

1	2	3	4	5	6	7	8	9	10
11			14	15	16	17	18	19	20
21			24	25	26	27	28	29	30
31			34	35	36	37	38	39	40
41			44	45	46	47	48	49	50
51			54	55	56	57	58	59	60
61			64	65	66	67	68	69	70
71			74	75	76	77	78	79	80
81			84	85	86	87	88	89	90
91			94	95	96	97	98	99	100

1. Count by threes to 30. Circle the numbers ▮ red ▷.

2. Count by twos to 30. Circle the numbers ▮ blue ▷.

REASONING

3. Continue the pattern.

1, 11, 21, 31, 41, _____, _____

Name _____ Date _____

Order to 100

Write the missing numbers.

1.
10 11 12 13 ___ 15 16 ___ 18

2.
___ 22 23 ___ 25 ___ ___ 28 ___ 30

3.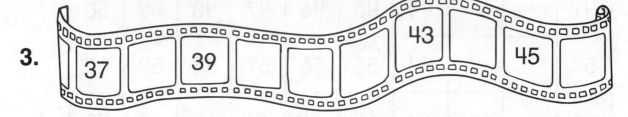
37 ___ 39 ___ ___ 43 ___ 45

4.
91 ___ ___ 94 95 96 ___ ___ ___ 100

5.
___ 52 ___ 54 ___ ___ ___ 58 59 ___

| STORY CORNER |

Read this riddle. Write the numbers.

6. We are numbers between 81 and 86.
   We come after 83.   _____ and _____

70

© Houghton Mifflin Harcourt Publishing Company

Unit 7
Core Skills Math, Grade 1

Name _____ Date _____

Numbers to 100

Write the missing numbers.

1.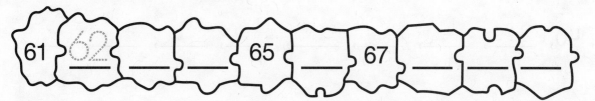

61 | 62 | ___ | ___ | 65 | ___ | 67 | ___ | ___ | ___

2.

56 | 57 | ___ | ___ | ___ | 61 | ___ | ___ | ___ | ___

3.

___ | ___ | 23 | 24 | ___ | ___ | ___ | ___ | ___ | 30

4.

45 | 46 | ___ | ___ | ___ | 50 | ___ | ___ | ___ | 54

5.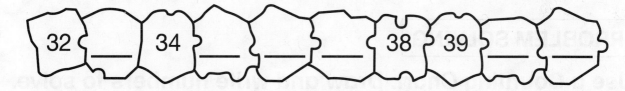

32 | ___ | 34 | ___ | ___ | ___ | 38 | 39 | ___

6.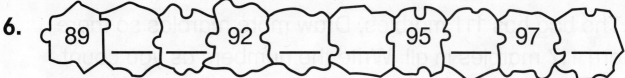

89 | ___ | ___ | 92 | ___ | ___ | 95 | ___ | 97 | ___

NUMBER SENSE

7. Circle the numbers that are less than 20.

15   16   17   18   19   20   21   22   23   24   25

71

Count by Ones to 120

Use a Counting Chart. Count forward. Write the numbers.

1. 40, _41_, _42_, _43_, _44_, _45_, _46_, _47_, _48_

2. 55, ____, ____, ____, ____, ____, ____, ____, ____

3. 37, ____, ____, ____, ____, ____, ____, ____, ____

4. 102, ____, ____, ____, ____, ____, ____, ____, ____

5. 96, ____, ____, ____, ____, ____, ____, ____, ____

PROBLEM SOLVING

Use a Counting Chart. Draw and write numbers to solve.

6. The bag has 111 marbles. Draw more marbles so there
are 117 marbles in all. Write the numbers as you count.

111

Count by Tens to 120

Use a Counting Chart. Count by tens. Write the numbers.

1. 1, __11__, __21__, __31__, __41__, __51__, __61__, __71__, __81__, __91__

2. 14, ___, ___, ___, ___, ___, ___, ___, ___, ___

3. 7, ___, ___, ___, ___, ___, ___, ___, ___, ___

4. 29, ___, ___, ___, ___, ___, ___, ___, ___, ___

5. 5, ___, ___, ___, ___, ___, ___, ___, ___, ___

6. 12, ___, ___, ___, ___, ___, ___, ___, ___, ___

7. 26, ___, ___, ___, ___, ___, ___, ___, ___, ___

8. 3, ___, ___, ___, ___, ___, ___, ___, ___, ___

9. 8, ___, ___, ___, ___, ___, ___, ___, ___, ___

PROBLEM SOLVING

Solve.

10. I am after 70.

I am before 90.

You say me when you count by tens.

What number am I? _____

Numbers from 100 to 110

Write the number.

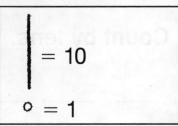

| = 10
o = 1

1.

_____

2.

_____

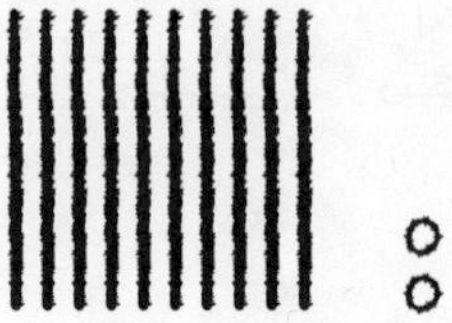

Use | to show the number. Write the number.
o

3. 10 tens and
6 more

4. 10 tens and
1 more

5. 10 tens and
9 more

_____   _____   _____

PROBLEM SOLVING

6. Solve to find the number of pens.

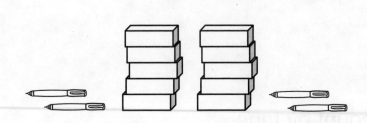

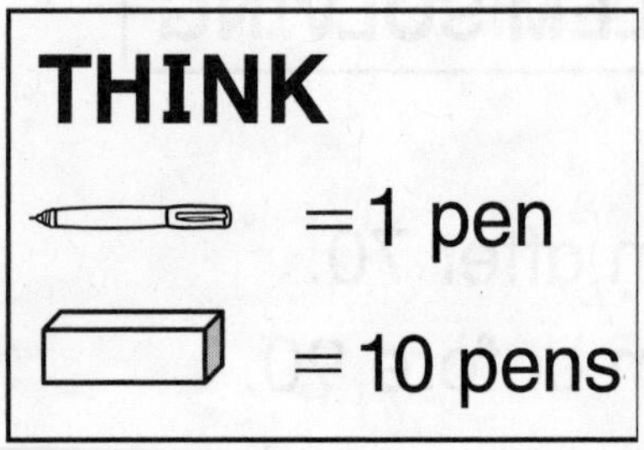

THINK

╱ = 1 pen

▭ = 10 pens

There are _____ pens.

Name _____ Date _____

Numbers from 110 to 120

Use | to model the number. Write the number.

1.

___114___

2.

_____

3.

_____

4.

_____

5.

_____

6.

_____

PROBLEM SOLVING

Choose a way to solve. Draw or write to explain.

7. Dave collects rocks. He makes 12 groups of 10 rocks and has none left over. How many rocks does Dave have?

_____ rocks

Show Numbers in Different Ways

Use ▭▭▭▭ ▫ **to show the number two different ways.**
Draw both ways.

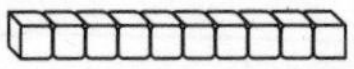

1.   62

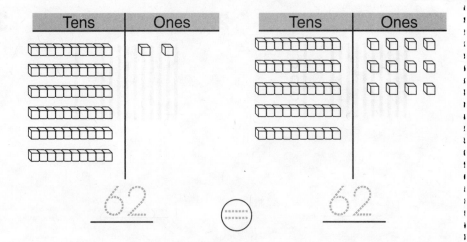

2.   38

Tens	Ones

Tens	Ones

_____ ○ _____

3.   47

Tens	Ones

Tens	Ones

_____ ○ _____

76

Adding and Subtracting

Work with a friend. You need connecting cubes.
Listen and do.

	Put in.	Put in.	Write the addition sentence.	Take away.	Write the subtraction sentence.
1.	3	4	3 + 4 = 7	4	7 - 4 = 3
2.	6	2		2	
3.	4	6		6	
4.	5	5		5	
5.	6	3		3	

STORY CORNER

6. Look at the picture.
Make up a story problem.
Tell it to a friend.

Write the number sentence. ____ ◯ ____ ═ ____

Name _____ Date _____

Counting On

Circle the greater number. Count on to add.

(7) 7,8
+ 1
8

2
+ (8) 8,9,10
10

(8) 8,9,10,11
+ 3
11

Circle the greater number. Write each sum.
Use counters to check.

1. (6)   3   3   8   7   3
 + 2   + 6   + 7   + 1   + 2   + 9
  8

2.   1   9   2   3   8   5
 + 9   + 2   + 8   + 5   + 3   + 2

3.   6   7   1   2   9   6
 + 1   + 3   + 7   + 9   + 3   + 3

REASONING

4. Evan has 10  in all.

How many are not shown?

_____

Name _____ Date _____

Doubles

Circle each double. Write each sum.

1. (3 + 3) = _6_   3 + 5 = _____   8 + 3 = _____

2. 4 + 2 = _____   6 + 6 = _____   4 + 4 = _____

3. 2 + 2 = _____   5 + 5 = _____   2 + 6 = _____

4.
1	1	3	2	3	6
+ 1	+ 7	+ 7	+ 8	+ 3	+ 3

5.
5	5	4	2	8	6
+ 3	+ 5	+ 4	+ 7	+ 3	+ 6

PROBLEM SOLVING

Solve. Write the addition sentence.

6. The cow jumped over the moon 4 times.
   Then it jumped 4 more times.
   How many times did it jump in all?

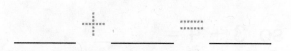
____ + ____ = ____

79

Doubles Plus One

Add. Use counters if you need to.

1.
$\begin{array}{r} 5 \\ +\ 5 \\ \hline 10 \end{array}$
$\begin{array}{r} 5 \\ +\ 6 \\ \hline \end{array}$
$\begin{array}{r} 2 \\ +\ 3 \\ \hline \end{array}$
$\begin{array}{r} 1 \\ +\ 1 \\ \hline \end{array}$
$\begin{array}{r} 4 \\ +\ 4 \\ \hline \end{array}$
$\begin{array}{r} 1 \\ +\ 2 \\ \hline \end{array}$

2.
$\begin{array}{r} 4 \\ +\ 5 \\ \hline \end{array}$
$\begin{array}{r} 3 \\ +\ 3 \\ \hline \end{array}$
$\begin{array}{r} 0 \\ +\ 0 \\ \hline \end{array}$
$\begin{array}{r} 3 \\ +\ 4 \\ \hline \end{array}$
$\begin{array}{r} 2 \\ +\ 2 \\ \hline \end{array}$
$\begin{array}{r} 0 \\ +\ 1 \\ \hline \end{array}$

NUMBER SENSE

**Do each one in your head.
Then write the sum.**

3. $4 + 4 = 8$,

so $4 + 5 = \underline{\ 9\ }$

4. $0 + 0 = 0$,

so $0 + 1 = \underline{\qquad}$

5. $2 + 2 = 4$,

so $2 + 3 = \underline{\qquad}$

6. $1 + 1 = 2$,

so $1 + 2 = \underline{\qquad}$

7. $5 + 5 = 10$,

so $5 + 6 = \underline{\qquad}$

8. $3 + 3 = 6$,

so $3 + 4 = \underline{\qquad}$

Unit 8
Core Skills Math, Grade 1

Order of Addends

$$\begin{array}{r} 7 \\ + 3 \\ \hline 10 \end{array} \qquad \begin{array}{r} 3 \\ + 7 \\ \hline 10 \end{array}$$

I see 4 and 4. That makes 8, and 1 more makes 9.

$$\begin{array}{r} 5 \\ + 4 \\ \hline 9 \end{array} \qquad \begin{array}{r} 4 \\ + 5 \\ \hline 9 \end{array}$$

Add.

1.
$$\begin{array}{r} 8 \\ + 2 \\ \hline \end{array} \qquad \begin{array}{r} 2 \\ + 8 \\ \hline \end{array} \qquad \begin{array}{r} 5 \\ + 5 \\ \hline \end{array} \qquad \begin{array}{r} 5 \\ + 6 \\ \hline \end{array} \qquad \begin{array}{r} 8 \\ + 1 \\ \hline \end{array} \qquad \begin{array}{r} 1 \\ + 8 \\ \hline \end{array}$$

2.
$$\begin{array}{r} 3 \\ + 3 \\ \hline \end{array} \qquad \begin{array}{r} 9 \\ + 3 \\ \hline \end{array} \qquad \begin{array}{r} 4 \\ + 4 \\ \hline \end{array} \qquad \begin{array}{r} 3 \\ + 9 \\ \hline \end{array} \qquad \begin{array}{r} 9 \\ + 2 \\ \hline \end{array} \qquad \begin{array}{r} 2 \\ + 9 \\ \hline \end{array}$$

VISUAL THINKING

3. Circle the correct answer.

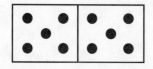

10

more than 10

less than 10

more than 10

less than 10

81

Adding and Subtracting

Do these in your head. Complete each table. Look for a pattern.

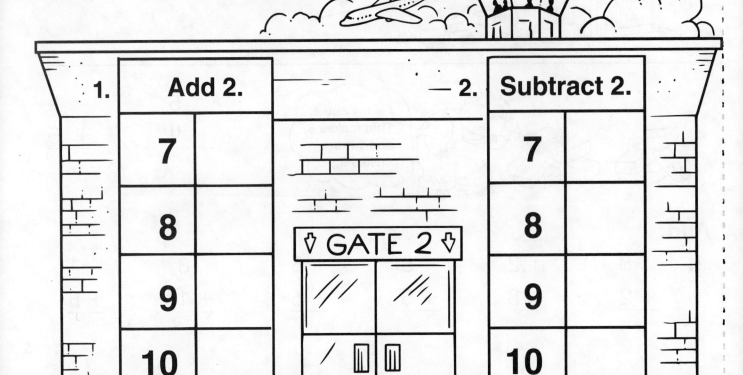

1. Add 2.		
7	
8	
9	
10	

— 2. Subtract 2.		
7	
8	
9	
10	

GATE 2

Match the pairs that have the same sum.

3. 2 + 6 •   • 7 + 3
    3 + 7 •   • 5 + 2
    2 + 5 •   • 6 + 2

4. 0 + 8 •   • 6 + 3
    2 + 8 •   • 8 + 0
    3 + 6 •   • 8 + 2

REASONING

Circle the answer.

5. Since 8 + 3 = 11,
   then 7 + ? = 11.

   4   5   6

6. Since 8 + 4 = 12,
   then 7 + ? = 12.

   3   4   5

Counting Back

$$10 \quad \boxed{10, 9}$$
$$\underline{-\ 1}$$
9

$$11 \quad \boxed{11, 10, 9, 8}$$
$$\underline{-\ 3}$$
8

$$10 \quad \boxed{10, 9, 8}$$
$$\underline{-\ 2}$$
8

Count back to subtract.

1.
$$\begin{array}{r} 11 \\ -\ 2 \\ \hline \end{array} \qquad \begin{array}{r} 8 \\ -\ 1 \\ \hline \end{array} \qquad \begin{array}{r} 9 \\ -\ 3 \\ \hline \end{array} \qquad \begin{array}{r} 7 \\ -\ 1 \\ \hline \end{array} \qquad \begin{array}{r} 8 \\ -\ 3 \\ \hline \end{array} \qquad \begin{array}{r} 10 \\ -\ 2 \\ \hline \end{array}$$

2.
$$\begin{array}{r} 10 \\ -\ 1 \\ \hline \end{array} \qquad \begin{array}{r} 11 \\ -\ 3 \\ \hline \end{array} \qquad \begin{array}{r} 12 \\ -\ 3 \\ \hline \end{array} \qquad \begin{array}{r} 9 \\ -\ 2 \\ \hline \end{array} \qquad \begin{array}{r} 7 \\ -\ 3 \\ \hline \end{array} \qquad \begin{array}{r} 8 \\ -\ 2 \\ \hline \end{array}$$

3.
$$\begin{array}{r} 9 \\ -\ 1 \\ \hline \end{array} \qquad \begin{array}{r} 10 \\ -\ 3 \\ \hline \end{array} \qquad \begin{array}{r} 7 \\ -\ 2 \\ \hline \end{array} \qquad \begin{array}{r} 6 \\ -\ 1 \\ \hline \end{array} \qquad \begin{array}{r} 12 \\ -\ 3 \\ \hline \end{array} \qquad \begin{array}{r} 6 \\ -\ 2 \\ \hline \end{array}$$

REASONING

4. Which has the greatest difference?
Circle it.

$$\begin{array}{r} 50 \\ -\ 3 \\ \hline \end{array} \qquad \begin{array}{r} 50 \\ -\ 2 \\ \hline \end{array} \qquad \begin{array}{r} 50 \\ -\ 1 \\ \hline \end{array}$$

83

Name _____ Date _____

Counting Up

Count up to subtract.

1.

$\begin{array}{r} 8 \\ -\ 7 \end{array}$ 7, **8** *(1 more)*

$\begin{array}{r} 11 \\ -\ 8 \end{array}$ 8, **9, 10, 11** *(3 more)*

$\begin{array}{r} 7 \\ -\ 5 \end{array}$ 5, **6, 7** *(2 more)*

$\begin{array}{r} 10 \\ -\ 7 \end{array}$ 7, **8, 9, 10** *(3 more)*

2.

$\begin{array}{r} 11 \\ -\ 9 \end{array}$ *(9, **10, 11**)*

$\begin{array}{r} 10 \\ -\ 8 \end{array}$ *(8, **9, 10**)*

$\begin{array}{r} 9 \\ -\ 8 \end{array}$ *(8, **9**)*

$\begin{array}{r} 12 \\ -\ 9 \end{array}$ *(9, **10, 11, 12**)*

3.

$\begin{array}{r} 10 \\ -\ 9 \end{array}$
$\begin{array}{r} 8 \\ -\ 6 \end{array}$
$\begin{array}{r} 6 \\ -\ 5 \end{array}$
$\begin{array}{r} 7 \\ -\ 4 \end{array}$
$\begin{array}{r} 9 \\ -\ 7 \end{array}$
$\begin{array}{r} 5 \\ -\ 3 \end{array}$

4.

$\begin{array}{r} 12 \\ -\ 8 \end{array}$
$\begin{array}{r} 5 \\ -\ 2 \end{array}$
$\begin{array}{r} 7 \\ -\ 6 \end{array}$
$\begin{array}{r} 10 \\ -\ 8 \end{array}$
$\begin{array}{r} 8 \\ -\ 5 \end{array}$
$\begin{array}{r} 6 \\ -\ 4 \end{array}$

REASONING

Use counting back or counting up to subtract.

5.

$\begin{array}{r} 11 \\ -\ 8 \end{array}$
$\begin{array}{r} 12 \\ -\ 3 \end{array}$
$\begin{array}{r} 9 \\ -\ 6 \end{array}$
$\begin{array}{r} 10 \\ -\ 2 \end{array}$
$\begin{array}{r} 8 \\ -\ 1 \end{array}$
$\begin{array}{r} 8 \\ -\ 6 \end{array}$

Circle the facts where you used counting up.

84

Name _____ Date _____

Addition and Subtraction

Add. Then subtract. Use counters to show.

1. 6 + 5 = __11__

11 − 5 = __6__

2. 7 + 4 = _____

11 − 4 = _____

3. 5 + 5 = _____

10 − 5 = _____

4. 8 + 4 = _____

12 − 4 = _____

5. 9 + 2 = _____

11 − 2 = _____

6. 6 + 6 = _____

12 − 6 = _____

7. 7 + 3 = _____

10 − 3 = _____

8. 7 + 5 = _____

12 − 5 = _____

PROBLEM SOLVING

Circle Add or Subtract.

9. A baker made 8 pies. Then he made
4 more. How many did he make in all?

Add   Subtract

85

Name _____ Date _____

Fact Families

Add or subtract. Circle the sentence that does not belong.

1. $3 + 7 = \underline{10}$

   $7 + 3 = \underline{10}$

   $6 + 3 = \underline{9}$

   $10 - 7 = \underline{3}$

   $10 - 3 = \underline{7}$

2. $1 + 8 = \underline{}$

   $8 + 1 = \underline{}$

   $9 - 8 = \underline{}$

   $8 - 1 = \underline{}$

   $9 - 1 = \underline{}$

3. $2 + 6 = \underline{}$

   $2 + 7 = \underline{}$

   $7 + 2 = \underline{}$

   $9 - 7 = \underline{}$

   $9 - 2 = \underline{}$

4. $5 + 3 = \underline{}$

   $3 + 5 = \underline{}$

   $8 - 5 = \underline{}$

   $9 - 5 = \underline{}$

   $8 - 3 = \underline{}$

REASONING

5. Write the difference. $13 - 5 = 8$, so $13 - 8 = \underline{}$

Add Three Numbers Using a Model

Look at the  **. Complete the addition sentences showing two ways to find the sum.**

1. 5 + 4 + 2 = _____

_____ + _____ = _____   _____ + _____ = _____

2. 2 + 2 + 6 = _____

 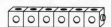   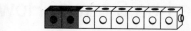

_____ + _____ = _____   _____ + _____ = _____

PROBLEM SOLVING

3. Choose three numbers from 1 to 6.
Write the numbers in an addition sentence.
Then show two ways to find the sum.

Name _____ Date _____

Problem Solving

CHOOSE THE OPERATION

Circle Add or Subtract.
Then write the number sentence.

1. Humpty Dumpty fell. 9 men came.
   Then 3 more came.
   How many men came in all?

   (Add)   Subtract

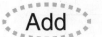

$$9 \; ⊕ \; 3 \; = \; 12$$

_12_ men

2. Little Boy Blue has 9 sheep.
   He has 5 cows. How many more
   sheep than cows does he have?

   Add   Subtract

   ___ ◯ ___ = ___

   _____ more sheep

3. Little Bo Peep had 11 sheep.
   She lost 3. How many sheep
   does she have left?

   Add   Subtract

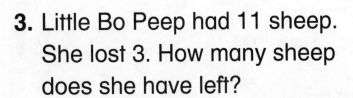

   ___ ◯ ___ = ___

   _____ sheep

STORY CORNER

4. Make up an addition or a
   subtraction story about the
   picture. Then solve.

Unit 8
Core Skills Math, Grade 1

Problem Solving

WRITE A NUMBER SENTENCE

Read each story. Then write a number sentence to solve.

1. The circus is coming.
   There are 5 young lions.
   There are 5 older lions.
   How many lions are there?

   $\underline{5} \;(\underline{+})\; \underline{5} = \underline{10}$

2. An elephant has 8 ribbons.
   A horse has 6 ribbons. How
   many more ribbons does the
   elephant have than the horse?

   _____ ◯ _____ = _____

3. A clown has 11 balloons.
   He pops 2 of them.
   How many balloons are left?

   _____ ◯ _____ = _____

STORY CORNER

4. Tell a story about the picture.
   Write a number sentence.

   _____ ◯ _____ = _____

89

Order Length

Draw three pencils in order from shortest to longest.

1. shortest

2.

3. longest

Draw three markers in order from longest to shortest.

4. shortest

5.

6. longest

PROBLEM SOLVING

Solve.

7. Fred has the shortest
toothbrush in the bathroom.
Circle Fred's toothbrush.

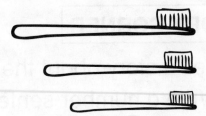

Unit 9

Core Skills Math, Grade 1

Indirect Measurement

Read the clues. Write <u>shorter</u> or <u>longer</u> to complete the sentence. Then draw to prove your answer.

1. Clue 1: A string is longer than a ribbon.

   Clue 2: The ribbon is longer than a crayon.

   So, the string is _____ than the crayon.

string	
ribbon	
crayon	

PROBLEM SOLVING

Solve. Draw or write to explain.

2. Megan's pencil is shorter
   than Tasha's pencil.

   Tasha's pencil is shorter
   than Kim's pencil.

   Is Megan's pencil shorter or
   longer than Kim's pencil?

   _____

Name _____ Date _____

Measuring in Nonstandard Units

Find these objects.

About how many 🖇 **long is each one?**

Estimate. Then use 🖇 **to measure.**

Objects	Estimate	Measurement
1.	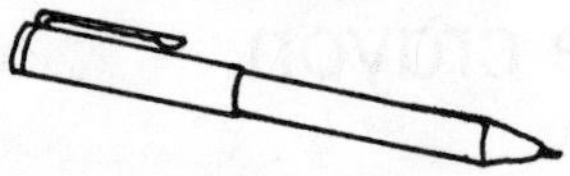 about ____ 🖇	about ____ 🖇
2.	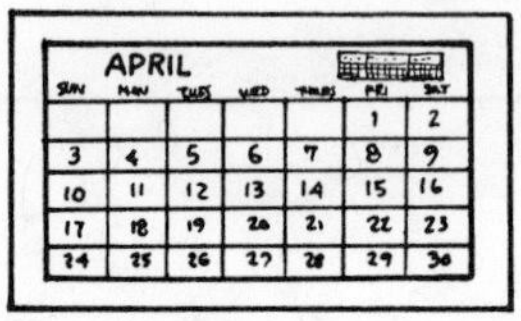 about ____ 🖇	about ____ 🖇
3.	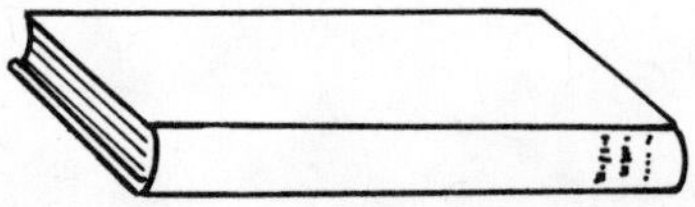 about ____ 🖇	about ____ 🖇
4.	 about ____ 🖇	about ____ 🖇

REASONING

5. What if you used a ✏ to measure the objects?

   Would you use more ✏ or more 🖇 ?

   Circle the answer.

   more ✏   more 🖇

Measuring Length

Use cubes to measure each brush. Write the length.

1.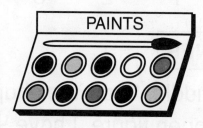

about _____ cubes

2.

about _____ cubes

3.

about _____ cubes

4.

about _____ cubes

REASONING

5. Circle the longer paint set.

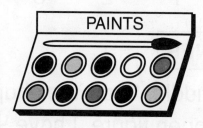

Name _____ Date _____

Problem Solving

MAKE A BAR GRAPH

Count the shapes. Complete the graph.

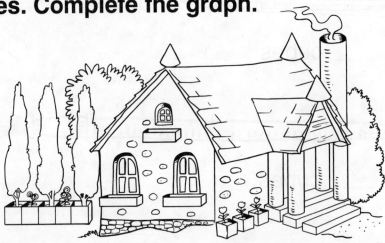

1.

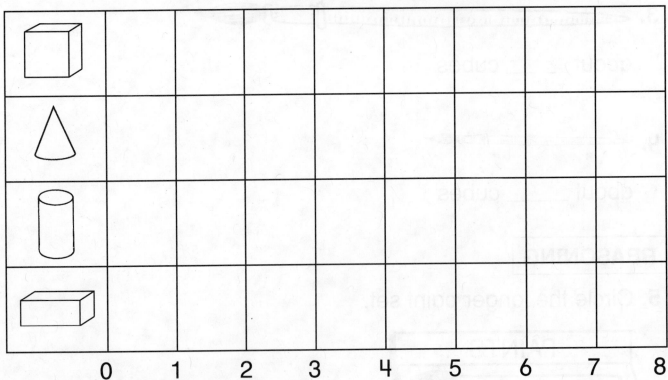

0   1   2   3   4   5   6   7   8

STORY CORNER

2. Read this riddle. Draw the shape.

I am an open figure. I have 4 sides.

I am a letter between T and X. _____

Unit 9
Core Skills Math, Grade 1

Problem Solving

MAKE AND USE A BAR GRAPH

Work with a group of ten friends. Ask which animal each friend in the group likes best. Use tally marks 卌 to count.

 kitten   pony    puppy   bunny

Color a ☐ **for each tally mark.**

1.

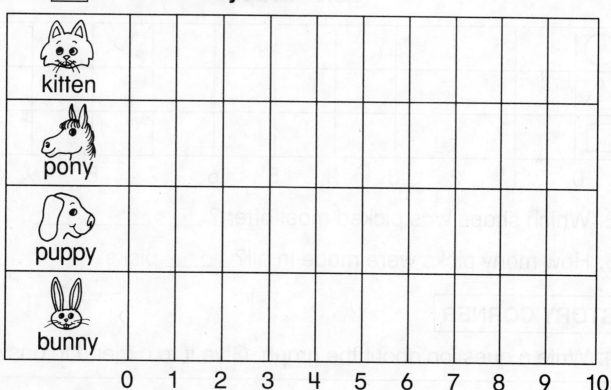

0 1 2 3 4 5 6 7 8 9 10

2. Which animal did your group like best? _____

3. How many in your group chose this animal? _____

4. Which animal did your group like the least? _____

Graphing Data

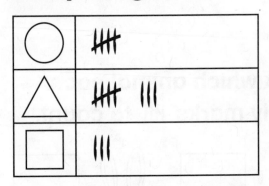

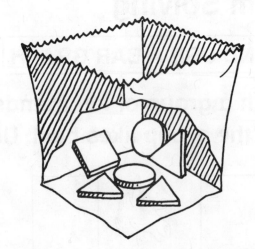

Read the table above.

1. Fill in the graph below to show how many times each shape was picked.

Color Graph

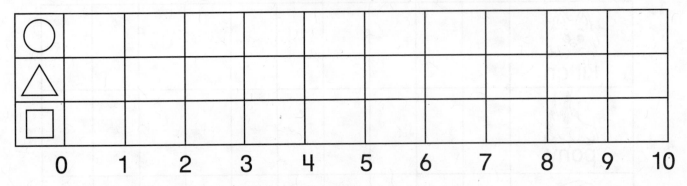

2. Which shape was picked most often? _____

3. How many picks were made in all? _____ picks

| **STORY CORNER** |

4. Write a question about the graph. Give it to a friend to answer.

_____

_ _

_ _

_ _

Name ______________________ Date ____________

Problem Solving

WRITE APPROPRIATE QUESTIONS

Some children counted birds they saw at a feeder. Then they made this table.

Birds at the Feeder			
Children	**First Week**	**Second Week**	**Third Week**
Joe	6	4	3
Lisa	4	4	2
Ken	5	2	4

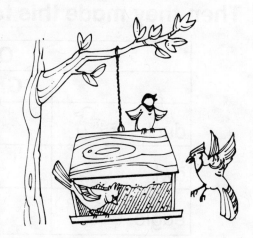

1. Read the table. Write a question about the table.

STORY CORNER

2. Write another question about the table.
Have your friend give the answer.

Problem Solving

MAKE A TABLE

Some children voted for their favorite birds.
Then they made this table.

Our Favorite Birds			
	Grade 1	Grade 2	Grade 3
duck	10	7	3
owl	12	13	7
eagle	9	8	15

Read the table. Answer these questions about it.

1. How many children in Grade 1 like ducks best? _10_ children

2. How many children in Grade 2 like owls best? ____ children

3. How many children in Grade 3 like eagles best? ____ children

4. How many children in all like ducks best? ____ children

STORY CORNER

5. Write a question about the table. Give it to a friend to answer.

_____

- -

_____

- -

_____

- -

_____

Problem Solving

WRITE APPROPRIATE QUESTIONS

This table shows how many books the
first-grade classes collected for a book sale.

Number of Books Collected					
Room Number	Reading	Science	Math	Social Studies	Geography
130	19	17	11	7	4
131	18	15	18	13	5
132	9	10	13	8	14

**Look at the table. Circle the questions
that you can answer by using the table.**

1. How many books did Room 133 collect?

   How many science books were collected?

2. Which room collected the most math books?

   How many music books did Room 132 collect?

3. Write a question that you can answer by using this table.

   _____

   _

   _____

   _

STORY CORNER

4. Make up other questions about this table. Tell them to a
   friend. Have your friend answer each question.

Name _____ Date _____

Fair Shares

Circle the ones that show fair shares.

1.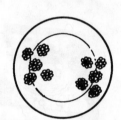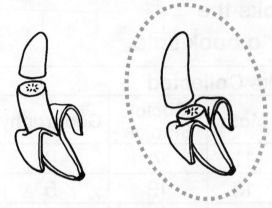

2.

3.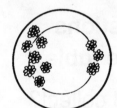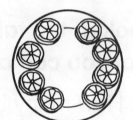

4.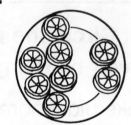

5.

6.

VISUAL THINKING

7. Rosa and Joe want fair shares of pizza.
   How should the pizza be cut?
   Draw a line to show. Your pizza
   should show equal parts.

100

Halves

Draw a line to show two equal parts.
Then color to show $\frac{1}{2}$.

1.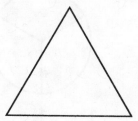

2.

3.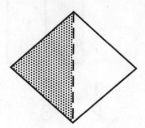

4.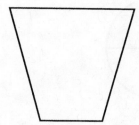

Find the shapes that show two equal parts. Color $\frac{1}{2}$.

5.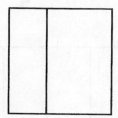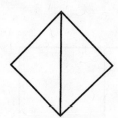

PROBLEM SOLVING

Solve.

6. Two squirrels shared 4 nuts.
Each had one half of the 4 nuts.
How many nuts did each squirrel have?

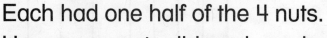

_____ nuts

Name _____ Date _____

Recognize Fourths

Circle the fraction that each shape shows.

1.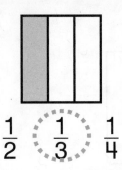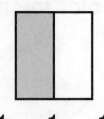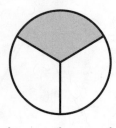

$\frac{1}{2}$ $\frac{1}{3}$ $\frac{1}{4}$ $\frac{1}{2}$ $\frac{1}{3}$ $\frac{1}{4}$ $\frac{1}{2}$ $\frac{1}{3}$ $\frac{1}{4}$

2.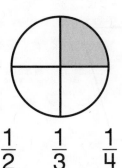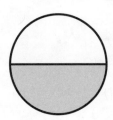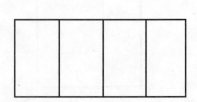

$\frac{1}{2}$ $\frac{1}{3}$ $\frac{1}{4}$ $\frac{1}{2}$ $\frac{1}{3}$ $\frac{1}{4}$ $\frac{1}{2}$ $\frac{1}{3}$ $\frac{1}{4}$

Find the shapes that show four equal parts. Color $\frac{1}{4}$.

3.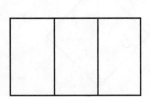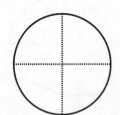

VISUAL THINKING

4. Which is greater, $\frac{1}{3}$ or $\frac{1}{4}$?

Circle the greater fraction.

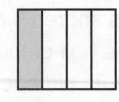 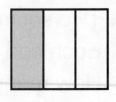

$\frac{1}{4}$ $\frac{1}{3}$

Unit 10
Core Skills Math, Grade 1

Show Fourths

Circle the shapes that show fourths.

1.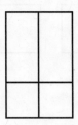

2.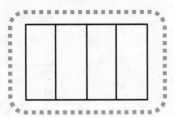

3.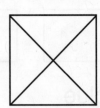

4.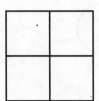

5.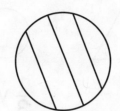

6.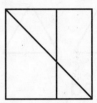

7.

8.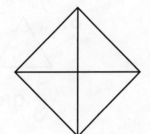

9.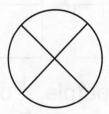

PROBLEM SOLVING

Solve.

10. Chad drew a picture to show a quarter of a circle. Which shape did Chad draw? Circle it.

Name _____ Date _____

Fractions in Groups

Color to show each fraction of a group.

1.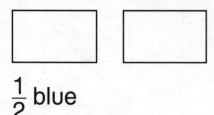

$\frac{1}{2}$ blue

2.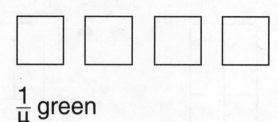

$\frac{1}{4}$ green

3.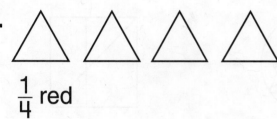

$\frac{1}{4}$ red

4.

$\frac{1}{3}$ yellow

5.

$\frac{1}{2}$ purple, $\frac{1}{2}$ orange

6.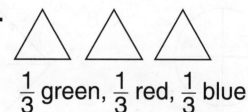

$\frac{1}{3}$ green, $\frac{1}{3}$ red, $\frac{1}{3}$ blue

NUMBER SENSE

7. There were 3 bears in all.
Write the fraction that tells
what part of the group is left.

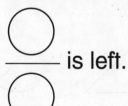 is left.

Unit 10
Core Skills Math, Grade 1

Name _____ Date _____

The Calendar

Complete the calendar for next month.

_____, 20 _____

Sunday	Monday	Tuesday	Wednesday	Thursday	Friday	Saturday

Use the calendar. Write the answers.

1. How many days are in this month? _____ days

2. Name the first day of this month. _____

3. Name the last day of this month. _____

4. What is today's date? _____

NUMBER SENSE

5. Look at calendars for this month and next month. Circle the answer.

Next month is _____? .

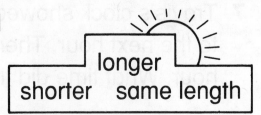

longer
shorter   same length

Unit 11
Core Skills Math, Grade 1

Reading the Clock

Show each time on your .
Trace the hour hand on each clock. Write the time.

1.

_____ o'clock

2.

_____ o'clock

3.

_____ o'clock

Show each time on your .
Trace the minute hand on each clock. Write the time.

4.

_____ o'clock

5.

_____ o'clock

6.

_____ o'clock

PROBLEM SOLVING

Use your .

7. Travis's clock showed 4 o'clock. Lee moved the short hand to the next hour. Then Nell moved the short hand to the next hour. What time did the clock show then?

_____ o'clock

106

Time to the Hour

Draw the hour hand so that both clocks show the same time.

1.

1:00   **5:00**   **11:00**

Write the time on the clock so that both clocks show the same time.

2.

NUMBER SENSE

3. Write the time on the clock so that it shows 1 hour later than 11 o'clock.

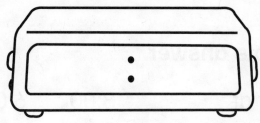

Unit 11
Core Skills Math, Grade 1

Hour Hand and Minute Hand

Draw the hour hand so that both clocks show the same time.

1.

5:00   **8:00**   **2:00**

Draw the minute hand so that both clocks show the same time.

2.

10:00   **3:00**   **6:00**

Draw the hour hand and the minute hand.

3.
  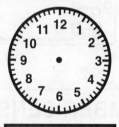

12:00   **9:00**   **1:00**

REASONING

Circle the reasonable answer.

4. Maria eats dinner at _____.   3:00   6:00

Understanding Time

HOUR

Read the time. Use a punch-out clock. Show 1 hour later.
Then draw hands on the clock to show 1 hour later.

1. `4:00`

2. `9:00`

3. `1:00`

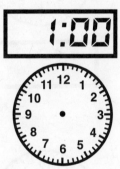

4. `10:00`

5. `5:00`

6. `11:00`

PROBLEM SOLVING

Solve. Write the answer.

7. The bus leaves in 1 hour. It is 2:00 now.
   What time will the bus leave?

   _____ : _____

Thirty Minutes

Write each time.

1.

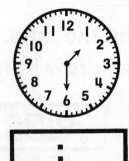

8:00

2.

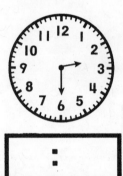

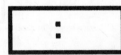

Show the time. Draw the minute hand.

3.

10:00

10:30

11:00

NUMBER SENSE

4. Circle the better estimate.
How long will the movie last?

more than 30 minutes
less than 30 minutes

110

Thirty Minutes: Half Hour

Write the times.

1.

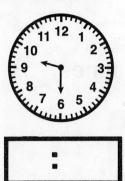

$$\boxed{\quad : \quad}$$

$$\boxed{\quad : \quad}$$

$$\boxed{\quad : \quad}$$

2.

$$\boxed{\quad : \quad}$$

$$\boxed{\quad : \quad}$$

$$\boxed{\quad : \quad}$$

3.

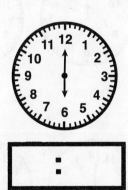

$$\boxed{\quad : \quad}$$

$$\boxed{\quad : \quad}$$

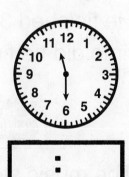

$$\boxed{\quad : \quad}$$

PROBLEM SOLVING

Solve. Write the answer.

4. The bus comes at 8:00. It takes 30 minutes to get to school.

What time will the bus get there? _____ **:**

111

Unit 11
Core Skills Math, Grade 1

Name _____ Date _____

Problem Solving

USE A MODEL

Use your to solve each problem.
Draw the hands on the clocks to show the times.

1.

Bob started drawing at 3:00.
He finished 1 hour later. At what
time did he finish?

2.

Greg started eating lunch at 12:00.
He finished 30 minutes later. At what
time did he finish?

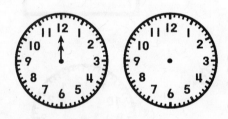

3.

The music started at 8:00. It lasted
2 hours. At what time did it end?

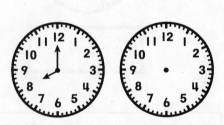

STORY CORNER

4. Make up a story about the pictures.
Share your story
with a friend.

112

Penny and Nickel

Circle how much money is needed.

1.

2.

3.

Count by fives. Circle how much money is needed.

4.

REASONING

Circle the one that costs less.

5.

6.

Unit 11
Core Skills Math, Grade 1

Counting Pennies

Write how much.

1.

_____3_____ ¢

2.

_____ ¢

3.

_____ ¢

4.

_____ ¢

5.

_____ ¢

6.

_____ ¢

REASONING

7. Look at each purse. Circle the purse that has more pennies. Draw an X on the purse that has fewer pennies.

Counting Pennies with Groups of 10

10 pennies

Count. Write how many pennies in all.

1.

_____

2.

_____

3.

_____

4.

_____

REASONING

5. Circle the greater amount of money.

Dime

Count by fives and tens. Circle how much money is needed.

1.

2.

3.

4.

5.

6.

NUMBER SENSE

7. Circle the greatest amount.

20 pennies   4 dimes   5 nickels

Quarter

Write each amount.
Then circle the ones that have the same value as a **.**

1.

_____ ¢

2.

_____ ¢

3.

_____ ¢

4.

_____ ¢

5.

_____ ¢

6.

_____ ¢

REASONING

7. Circle the amount that you can show
with the least number of coins.   15¢   20¢   25¢

Name _____ Date _____

Equal and Not Equal

Which are true? Circle your answers.
Which are false? Cross out your answers.

1. $6 + 4 = 5 + 5$ **2.** $10 = 6 - 4$

3. $8 + 8 = 16 - 8$ **4.** $14 = 1 + 4$

5. $8 - 0 = 12 - 4$ **6.** $17 = 9 + 8$

7. $8 + 3 = 8 - 3$ **8.** $15 - 6 = 6 + 9$

9. $12 = 5 + 5 + 2$ **10.** $7 + 6 = 6 + 7$

11. $5 - 4 = 4 + 5$ **12.** $0 + 9 = 9 - 0$

PROBLEM SOLVING

13. Which are true? Use a ▭▷ to circle.

$15 = 15$ $12 = 2$ $3 = 8 - 5$

$15 = 1 + 5$ $9 + 2 = 2 + 9$ $9 + 2 = 14$

$1 + 2 + 3 = 3 + 3$ $5 - 3 = 5 + 3$ $13 = 8 + 5$

Missing Numbers

Write the missing numbers. Use 🎲 🎲 if you need to.

1. $6 + \boxed{7} = 13$

$13 - 6 = \boxed{7}$

2. $9 + \boxed{} = 14$

$14 - 9 = \boxed{}$

3. $\boxed{} + 7 = 15$

$15 - 7 = \boxed{}$

4. $\boxed{} + 3 = 12$

$12 - \boxed{} = 3$

5. $\boxed{} = 9 + 8$

$8 = \boxed{} - 9$

6. $\boxed{} = 8 + 8$

$8 = \boxed{} - 8$

PROBLEM SOLVING

Use cubes or draw a picture to solve.

7. Sally has 9 toy trucks. She gets 3 more toy trucks.
How many toy trucks does she have now?

_____ toy trucks

Use Related Facts

Write the missing numbers.

1. Find 16 − 9.

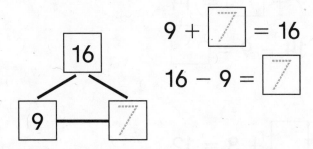

$9 + \boxed{} = 16$

$16 - 9 = \boxed{}$

2. Find 12 − 7.

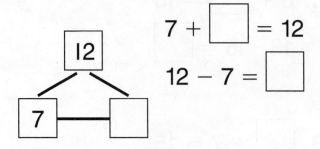

$7 + \boxed{} = 12$

$12 - 7 = \boxed{}$

3. Find 15 − 6.

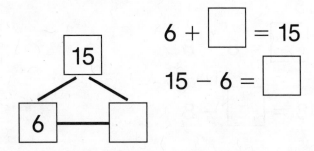

$6 + \boxed{} = 15$

$15 - 6 = \boxed{}$

4. Find 18 − 9.

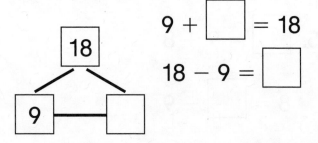

$9 + \boxed{} = 18$

$18 - 9 = \boxed{}$

PROBLEM SOLVING

Look at the shapes in the addition sentence. Draw a shape to show a related subtraction fact.

5.

⬛ + ⬜ = ◼   ◼ − _____ = ⬛

120

Choosing Addition or Subtraction

Complete each number sentence. Write + or − in the ◯ .

1. 9 ◯ 4 = 5

2. 5 ◯ 4 = 9

3. 12 ◯ 7 = 5

4. 7 ◯ 4 = 11

5. 11 ◯ 8 = 3

6. 12 ◯ 7 = 5

7. 8 ◯ 4 = 12

8. 6 ◯ 6 = 12

Solve.

9. Ling ate 3 crackers from a new box.
The box had 14 crackers when it was
opened. How many crackers are left?   _____ crackers

STORY CORNER

10. Make up a story problem about the
picture. Give it to a friend to solve.

Name _____ Date _____

Missing Addends

Complete each number sentence.
Write the missing addend.

1. $3 + \underline{9} = 12$

2. $5 + \underline{} = 11$

3. $7 + \underline{} = 8$

4. $6 + \underline{} = 10$

5. $2 + \underline{} = 7$

6. $7 + \underline{} = 10$

7. $6 + \underline{} = 12$

8. $4 + \underline{} = 6$

9. $9 + \underline{} = 11$

10. $5 + \underline{} = 12$

Solve.

11. Hal runs 6 miles one day. His total
after two days is 11 miles. How
many miles does he run
the second day?

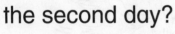 _____ miles

---

REASONING

Circle the answer.

12. If $10 + 7 = 17$, then what is $9 + 7$?

     16   17   18

Tens and Ones

Circle groups of ten. Write how many stars in all.

1.

_____ stars

2.

_____ stars

3.

_____ stars

4.

_____ stars

NUMBER SENSE • ESTIMATION

About how many beans are in each jar?
Circle the better estimate.

60 beans

5.

more than 30

fewer than 30

6.

between 40 and 60

between 10 and 30

Ten Less, Ten More

Use mental math. Complete the chart.

	Ten Less		Ten More
1.	38	48	58
2.	_____	25	_____
3.	_____	73	_____
4.	_____	89	_____
5.	8	_____	_____
6.	_____	_____	47

PROBLEM SOLVING

Choose a way to solve. Draw or write to show your work.

7. Jim has 16 pennies. Doug has 10 fewer pennies than Jim. How many pennies does Doug have?

_____ pennies

124

Adding Tens

Add tens. Write each addition sentence.

1.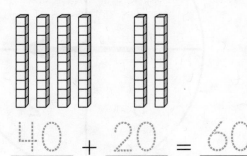

$$\underline{40} + \underline{20} = \underline{60}$$

2.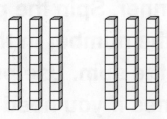

___ + ___ = ___

3.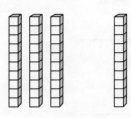

___ + ___ = ___

4.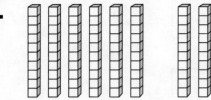

___ + ___ = ___

5.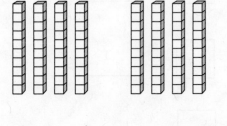

___ + ___ = ___

6.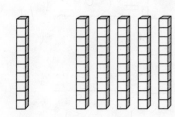

___ + ___ = ___

NUMBER SENSE

Do these in your head. Match the pairs to their sums.

7. 7 + 1 •   • 30

20 + 10 •   • 6

2 + 4 •   • 8

8. 40 + 30 •   • 40

20 + 20 •   • 9

5 + 4 •   • 70

Exploring 2-Digit Addition

Use a pencil and a paper clip to make a spinner. Spin the paper clip. Write the number in the box. Add. Write the sum. Use punch-out tens and ones if you need to.

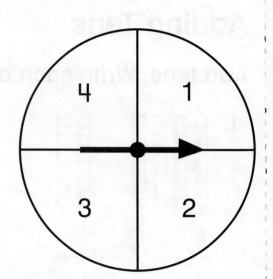

1. 54 + [3] = 57

2. 91 + [ ] = _____

3. 65 + [ ] = _____

4. 32 + [ ] = _____

5. 73 + [ ] = _____

6. 40 + [ ] = _____

7. 81 + [ ] = _____

8. 24 + [ ] = _____

9. 50 + [ ] = _____

10. 62 + [ ] = _____

STORY CORNER

Solve the riddle.

11. I am 1 more than 3 tens and 6 ones. What number am I?

_____

12. I am 1 more than 3 tens and 7 ones. What number am I?

_____

Use a Hundred Chart to Add

Use the hundred chart to add.
Count on by ones or tens.

1. 47 + 2 = _49_

2. 26 + 50 = _____

3. 22 + 5 = _____

4. 40 + 4 = _____

5. 4 + 85 = _____

1	2	3	4	5	6	7	8	9	10
11	12	13	14	15	16	17	18	19	20
21	22	23	24	25	26	27	28	29	30
31	32	33	34	35	36	37	38	39	40
41	42	43	44	45	46	47	48	49	50
51	52	53	54	55	56	57	58	59	60
61	62	63	64	65	66	67	68	69	70
71	72	73	74	75	76	77	78	79	80
81	82	83	84	85	86	87	88	89	90
91	92	93	94	95	96	97	98	99	100

PROBLEM SOLVING

Choose a way to solve. Draw or write to show your work.

6. 17 children are on the bus. Then 20 more children get on the bus. How many children are on the bus now?

_____ children

Use Models to Add

Use ⬛⬛⬛⬛⬛⬛ ⬛. Add the ones or tens. Write the sum.

1. $44 + 5 =$ _49_

2. $16 + 70 =$ _____

3. $78 + 20 =$ _____

4. $52 + 7 =$ _____

5. $2 + 13 =$ _____

6. $73 + 4 =$ _____

7. $84 + 3 =$ _____

8. $20 + 25 =$ _____

9. $49 + 30 =$ _____

10. $81 + 8 =$ _____

PROBLEM SOLVING

Solve. Draw or write to explain.

11. Maria has 21 marbles.

She buys a bag of 20 marbles.

How many marbles does Maria have now?

_____ marbles

Make Ten to Add

Use ▭▭▭▭▭ ▯. Draw to show how you make a ten. Find the sum.

1. 26 + 5 = __31__

2. 68 + 4 = _____

3. 35 + 8 = _____

PROBLEM SOLVING

Choose a way to solve. Draw or write to show your work.

4. Debbie has 27 markers.
Sal has 9 markers.
How many markers do they have?

_____ markers

Name _____ Date _____

Use Place Value to Add

Draw a quick picture. Use tens and ones to add.

1.   31
      + 26

Tens	Ones

3 tens + 1 one
2 tens + 6 ones
_____

_____ tens + _____ ones

_____ + _____ = _____

      31
    + 26

---

2.   54
      + 34

Tens	Ones

5 tens + 4 ones
3 tens + 4 ones
_____

_____ tens + _____ ones

_____ + _____ = _____

      54
    + 34

PROBLEM SOLVING

3. Write an addition sentence you can use to find the sum.
Then solve.

Addend   **Addend**

 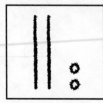

_____ + _____ = _____

Unit 13
Core Skills Math, Grade 1

Subtracting Tens

Add or subtract.

1.

70	50	80	60	40
+ 10	+ 20	− 30	− 20	+ 30
80				

2.

80	60	70	40	50
− 20	− 40	+ 20	− 20	+ 40

3.

80	60	70	60	80
+ 10	+ 30	− 40	− 30	− 10

NUMBER SENSE

Do these in your head. Look for a pattern.

4.

43	53	63	73	83
+ 10	+ 10	+ 10	+ 10	+ 10

5.

43	53	63	73	83
− 10	− 10	− 10	− 10	− 10

Add Three Numbers Using Grouping

Use groups to add two ways.
Complete the addition sentences.

1. 3 + 2 + 4 = _____

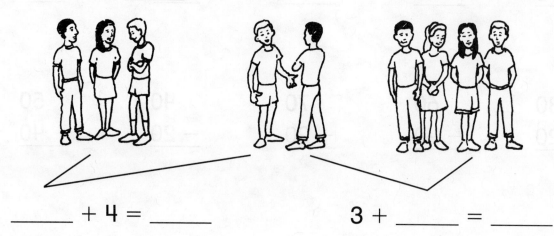

_____ + 4 = _____   3 + _____ = _____

2. 5 + 1 + 4 = _____

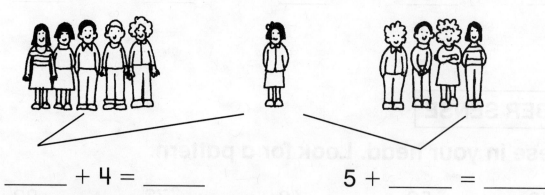

_____ + 4 = _____   5 + _____ = _____

STORY CORNER

3. Make up a story problem
about this picture.
Give it to a friend
to solve.

132

Using Doubles

Add or subtract. Use counters.

1.
$$\begin{array}{r} 1 \\ +\,1 \\ \hline 2 \end{array} \qquad \begin{array}{r} 2 \\ -\,1 \\ \hline 1 \end{array} \qquad \bigg| \qquad \begin{array}{r} 2 \\ +\,2 \\ \hline \end{array} \qquad \begin{array}{r} 4 \\ -\,2 \\ \hline \end{array} \qquad \bigg| \qquad \begin{array}{r} 3 \\ +\,3 \\ \hline \end{array} \qquad \begin{array}{r} 6 \\ -\,3 \\ \hline \end{array}$$

2.
$$\begin{array}{r} 4 \\ +\,4 \\ \hline \end{array} \qquad \begin{array}{r} 8 \\ -\,4 \\ \hline \end{array} \qquad \bigg| \qquad \begin{array}{r} 5 \\ +\,5 \\ \hline \end{array} \qquad \begin{array}{r} 10 \\ -\,5 \\ \hline \end{array} \qquad \bigg| \qquad \begin{array}{r} 6 \\ +\,6 \\ \hline \end{array} \qquad \begin{array}{r} 12 \\ -\,6 \\ \hline \end{array}$$

NUMBER SENSE

Try these in your head.

3.
$$\begin{array}{r} 7 \\ +\,7 \\ \hline \end{array} \qquad \begin{array}{r} 14 \\ -\,7 \\ \hline \end{array} \qquad \bigg| \qquad \begin{array}{r} 8 \\ +\,8 \\ \hline \end{array} \qquad \begin{array}{r} 16 \\ -\,8 \\ \hline \end{array} \qquad \bigg| \qquad \begin{array}{r} 9 \\ +\,9 \\ \hline \end{array} \qquad \begin{array}{r} 18 \\ -\,9 \\ \hline \end{array}$$

Name _____ Date _____

Doubles Plus One

Do these in your head. Then write the sums.

1. 1 + 1 = 2, so 1 + 2 = _3___ .

2. 4 + 4 = 8, so 4 + 5 = _____ .

3. 0 + 0 = 0, so 0 + 1 = _____ .

Write the sums.

4. 8 + 8 = _____, so 8 + 9 = _____ .

5. 7 + 7 = _____, so 7 + 8 = _____ .

Look for doubles to find the sums.

6.
5	3	6	4	2	3
+ 5	+ 3	+ 7	+ 5	+ 2	+ 4

7.
2	8	5	8	4	6
+ 3	+ 8	+ 6	+ 9	+ 4	+ 6

REASONING

Write the sums.

8. 5 + 5 = 10, so 5 + 6 = _____ .

9. 6 + 6 = 12, so 6 + 7 = _____ .

Unit 14
Core Skills Math, Grade 1

Doubles Minus One

Do these in your head. Then write the sums.

1. 4 + 4 = 8, so 4 + 3 = ___7___ .

2. 7 + 7 = 14, so 7 + 6 = _____ .

3. 8 + 8 = 16, so 8 + 7 = _____ .

4. 9 + 9 = 18, so 9 + 8 = _____ .

5. 6 + 6 = 12, so 6 + 5 = _____ .

Look for doubles to find the sums.

6.
```
   9      7      4      1      9      7
  +9     +6     +3     +1     +8     +7
```

7.
```
   8      1      5      8      4      5
  +8     +0     +4     +7     +4     +5
```

NUMBER SENSE

8. Circle 5 + 5 | red |▷ .

Circle 5 + 4 | blue |▷ .

Circle 5 + 6 | green |▷ .

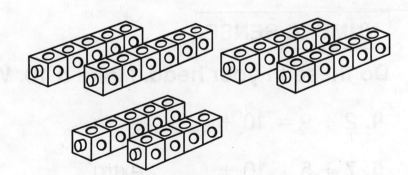

© Houghton Mifflin Harcourt Publishing Company

Make a 10

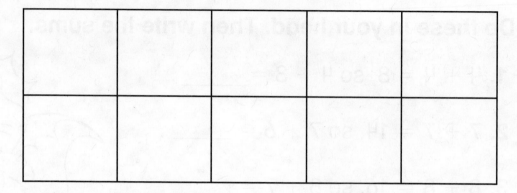

Use counters and the 10-frame.

Start with the greater number. Make a 10. Then add.

1.
$$\begin{array}{r}7\\+4\\\hline 11\end{array}\qquad\begin{array}{r}8\\+6\\\hline\end{array}\qquad\begin{array}{r}3\\+9\\\hline\end{array}\qquad\begin{array}{r}4\\+8\\\hline\end{array}\qquad\begin{array}{r}5\\+9\\\hline\end{array}\qquad\begin{array}{r}9\\+4\\\hline\end{array}$$

2.
$$\begin{array}{r}9\\+6\\\hline\end{array}\qquad\begin{array}{r}3\\+8\\\hline\end{array}\qquad\begin{array}{r}7\\+5\\\hline\end{array}\qquad\begin{array}{r}2\\+9\\\hline\end{array}\qquad\begin{array}{r}5\\+8\\\hline\end{array}\qquad\begin{array}{r}9\\+7\\\hline\end{array}$$

3.
$$\begin{array}{r}6\\+8\\\hline\end{array}\qquad\begin{array}{r}4\\+9\\\hline\end{array}\qquad\begin{array}{r}7\\+9\\\hline\end{array}\qquad\begin{array}{r}4\\+7\\\hline\end{array}\qquad\begin{array}{r}8\\+3\\\hline\end{array}\qquad\begin{array}{r}5\\+7\\\hline\end{array}$$

NUMBER SENSE

Do these in your head. Make a 10. Write how many extra.

4. $2 + 9 = 10 +$ _____ extra

5. $7 + 5 = 10 +$ _____ extra

Adding Three Numbers

Use a spinner. Spin.
Write the number in the box. Find the sum.

1.
```
   2        6        5
   2        4        5
 +[  ]    +[  ]    +[  ]
———      ———      ———
```

2.
```
   3        4        1
   7        4        9
 +[  ]    +[  ]    +[  ]
———      ———      ———
```

3.
```
  2      1      8      3      6      7
  8      1      2      3      6      3
+[ ]   +[ ]   +[ ]   +[ ]   +[ ]   +[ ]
——     ——     ——     ——     ——     ——
```

REASONING

Circle the one in each pair that you think
has the greater sum. Then solve to check.

4.
```
    7        8
    3        2
  + 6      + 5
  ———      ———
```

5.
```
    4        3
    4        4
  + 2      + 4
  ———      ———
```

Name _____ Date _____

Mental Math: Order and Zero

Find the sum.

1.
$$\begin{array}{r} 5 \\ +\,0 \\ \hline \end{array}$$
$$\begin{array}{r} 0 \\ +\,5 \\ \hline \end{array}$$
$$\begin{array}{r} 0 \\ +\,7 \\ \hline \end{array}$$
$$\begin{array}{r} 7 \\ +\,0 \\ \hline \end{array}$$
$$\begin{array}{r} 0 \\ +\,9 \\ \hline \end{array}$$
$$\begin{array}{r} 9 \\ +\,0 \\ \hline \end{array}$$

2.
$$\begin{array}{r} 8 \\ +\,0 \\ \hline \end{array}$$
$$\begin{array}{r} 0 \\ +\,8 \\ \hline \end{array}$$
$$\begin{array}{r} 8 \\ +\,8 \\ \hline \end{array}$$
$$\begin{array}{r} 0 \\ +\,0 \\ \hline \end{array}$$
$$\begin{array}{r} 4 \\ +\,4 \\ \hline \end{array}$$
$$\begin{array}{r} 4 \\ +\,0 \\ \hline \end{array}$$

3.
$$\begin{array}{r} 5 \\ +\,7 \\ \hline \end{array}$$
$$\begin{array}{r} 7 \\ +\,5 \\ \hline \end{array}$$
$$\begin{array}{r} 2 \\ +\,8 \\ \hline \end{array}$$
$$\begin{array}{r} 8 \\ +\,2 \\ \hline \end{array}$$
$$\begin{array}{r} 3 \\ +\,9 \\ \hline \end{array}$$
$$\begin{array}{r} 9 \\ +\,3 \\ \hline \end{array}$$

PROBLEM SOLVING

Solve.

4. Lillian threw fish to two penguins.
All the fish were caught. One penguin
caught 7 fish. The other penguin
caught no fish. How many fish
did Lillian throw?

_____ fish

138

Think Addition to Subtract

Use 🎲 🎲 to add and to subtract.

1.   9
   − 3
   ___
    ?

Think
   3
 + ⬜(6)
   ___
    9

So
   9
 − 3
 ___
  6

2. 15
   − 8
   ___
    ?

Think
   8
 + ⬜
   ___
   15

So
  15
 − 8
 ___

3. 11
   − 7
   ___
    ?

Think
   7
 + ⬜
   ___
   11

So
  11
 − 7
 ___

4. 13
   − 4
   ___
    ?

Think
   4
 + ⬜
   ___
   13

So
  13
 − 4
 ___

5. 14
   − 6
   ___
    ?

Think
   6
 + ⬜
   ___
   14

So
  14
 − 6
 ___

PROBLEM SOLVING

6. Write a number sentence to solve.
   I have 18 pieces of fruit. 9 are apples.
   The rest are oranges.
   How many are oranges?

_____ oranges

Sums and Differences to 14

Write the addition facts that help.
Then complete the subtraction facts.

1.

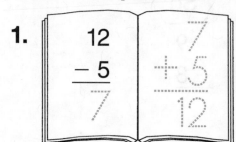

```
 12        7
- 5      + 5
---      ----
 7        12
```

```
 14
- 5
----
```

```
 10
- 6
----
```

2.

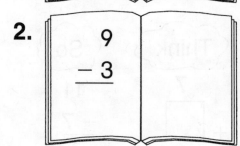

```
  9
- 3
----
```

```
 13
- 8
----
```

```
 11
- 4
----
```

3.

```
 12
- 8
----
```

```
 14
- 7
----
```

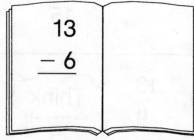

```
 13
- 6
----
```

4.

```
 11
- 9
----
```

```
  8
- 6
----
```

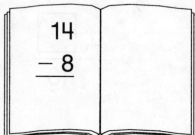

```
 14
- 8
----
```

PROBLEM SOLVING

5. Jon filled 4 bags with leaves. His mother filled 5 bags. How many bags in all did they fill?

_____ bags

6. Mollie washed 12 glasses. Her brother washed 6 glasses. How many more glasses did Mollie wash?

_____ more glasses

Sums and Differences to 18

Write the sum and difference for each pair.

1.
$$\begin{array}{r} 4 \\ + 8 \\ \hline 12 \end{array} \qquad \begin{array}{r} 12 \\ - 8 \\ \hline 4 \end{array} \qquad \bigg| \qquad \begin{array}{r} 8 \\ + 8 \\ \hline \end{array} \qquad \begin{array}{r} 16 \\ - 8 \\ \hline \end{array} \qquad \bigg| \qquad \begin{array}{r} 8 \\ + 5 \\ \hline \end{array} \qquad \begin{array}{r} 13 \\ - 5 \\ \hline \end{array}$$

2.
$$\begin{array}{r} 9 \\ + 8 \\ \hline \end{array} \qquad \begin{array}{r} 17 \\ - 8 \\ \hline \end{array} \qquad \bigg| \qquad \begin{array}{r} 7 \\ + 8 \\ \hline \end{array} \qquad \begin{array}{r} 15 \\ - 8 \\ \hline \end{array} \qquad \bigg| \qquad \begin{array}{r} 2 \\ + 9 \\ \hline \end{array} \qquad \begin{array}{r} 11 \\ - 9 \\ \hline \end{array}$$

3.
$$\begin{array}{r} 7 \\ + 7 \\ \hline \end{array} \qquad \begin{array}{r} 14 \\ - 7 \\ \hline \end{array} \qquad \bigg| \qquad \begin{array}{r} 6 \\ + 9 \\ \hline \end{array} \qquad \begin{array}{r} 15 \\ - 9 \\ \hline \end{array} \qquad \bigg| \qquad \begin{array}{r} 9 \\ + 9 \\ \hline \end{array} \qquad \begin{array}{r} 18 \\ - 9 \\ \hline \end{array}$$

REASONING

Which way would you use to find each sum?
Draw a line to match.

4. $9 + 7 = ?$ •   • Add doubles.

5. $9 + 2 = ?$ •   • Count on.

6. $6 + 6 = ?$ •   • Make a 10.

Fact Families

Write each fact family.

1.

$$6 + 7 = 13 \quad | \quad 7 + 6 = 13$$
$$13 - 7 = 6 \quad | \quad 13 - 6 = 7$$

2.

____ + ____ = ____ | ____ + ____ = ____

____ − ____ = ____ | ____ − ____ = ____

3.

____ + ____ = ____ | ____ + ____ = ____

____ − ____ = ____ | ____ − ____ = ____

4.

____ + ____ = ____ | ____ + ____ = ____

____ − ____ = ____ | ____ − ____ = ____

REASONING

Circle an estimate. Then use a to solve.

5. There are 9 children swimming.
8 more come. Then 10 of them leave.
How many children are swimming?

more than 9

fewer than 9

_____ children

Unit 14
Core Skills Math, Grade 1

Name _____ Date _____

Use Think Addition to Subtract

Think of an addition fact to help you subtract.

1. 13
      $-\ 8$

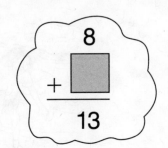

8
+ □
13

2. 12
      $-\ 6$

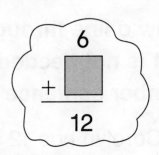

6
+ □
12

3. 6
      $-\ 4$

4. 14
      $-\ 9$

5. 9
      $-\ 5$

6. 13
      $-\ 6$

7. 10
      $-\ 7$

8. 12
      $-\ 4$

9. 16
      $-\ 7$

10. 11
       $-\ 8$

11. 14
       $-\ 8$

12. 15
       $-\ 7$

PROBLEM SOLVING

Solve. Draw or write to show your work.

13. I have 15 nickels.

Some are old.

6 are new.

How many nickels are old?

_____ nickels

Unit 14
Core Skills Math, Grade 1

Problem Solving

| TOO MUCH INFORMATION: ADDITION AND SUBTRACTION |

Draw a line through the sentence that is not needed. Then write a number sentence to solve.

1. Carolyn has 12 sea plants.

~~Eddie has 6 sea plants.~~

Carolyn gives Jim 5 plants.

How many plants does

she have left?

$12 \bigcirc 5 = 7$

_____ 7 _____ plants

2. There are 9 men fishing.

There are 8 women fishing.

There are 12 boats.

How many people are fishing?

____ $\bigcirc$ ____ = ____

_____ people

3. Marta has 10 clams.

Today Marta found 4 crabs.

Marta has 6 fish.

How many more clams

does she have than fish?

____ $\bigcirc$ ____ = ____

_____ more clams

| STORY CORNER |

4. Tell a story about the picture.

Write a number sentence.

____ $\bigcirc$ ____ = ____

Unit 14
Core Skills Math, Grade 1

More Adding Three Numbers

**Choose a strategy. Circle two addends
to add first. Write the sum.**

1.　(7)
　　(3)
　　+ 3
　　‾‾‾‾
　　13

2.　　2
　　　2
　　+ 6
　　‾‾‾‾

3.　　6
　　　6
　　+ 3
　　‾‾‾‾

4.　　2
　　　0
　　+ 8
　　‾‾‾‾

5.　　1
　　　2
　　+ 9
　　‾‾‾‾

6.　　6
　　　4
　　+ 3
　　‾‾‾‾

7.　　3
　　　3
　　+ 5
　　‾‾‾‾

8.　　4
　　　4
　　+ 8
　　‾‾‾‾

PROBLEM SOLVING

Draw a picture. Write the number sentence.

9. Don has 4 black dogs.
   Tim has 3 small dogs.
   Sue has 3 big dogs.
   How many dogs do they have?

_____ + _____ + _____ = _____ dogs

Answer Key

Page 1

Circle birds, rabbits, squirrels, and turtles.

1. 2
2. 1
3. 3
4. Circle first picture.

Page 2

1. 5, 4, 5
2. 4, 3, 5
3. 2, 4, 3
4. Circle middle group. Draw an X on the first and last groups.

Page 3

1. 3
2. 0
3. 2
4. 0
5. 1
6. 4
7. Circle middle group. Draw an X on the first and last groups.

Page 4

1. 6, six
2. 4, four
3. 0, zero
4. 5, five
5. 7, seven
6. 3, three
7. Circle second and last groups. Draw an X on the first and third groups.

Page 5

1. Circle second, fourth, and sixth groups.
2. Circle first, third, and fifth groups.
3. Circle first group.

Page 6

1. nine, 9
2. seven, 7
3. ten, 10
4. eight, 8
5. Circle middle group.

Page 7

1. Circle 6, 5
2. 4, circle 9
3. 5, circle 3
4. Circle 7, 9
5. six
6. ten

Page 8

1. Check drawings. 5 squares, 3 triangles, 1 rectangle, 4 circles
2. Circle square.
3. Circle rectangle.

Page 9

1. 4, 1; 5
2. 2, 1; 3
3. 5, 1; 6
4. 4
5. 5

Page 10

1. $2 + 1 = 3$
2. $2 + 2 = 4$
3. $4 + 1 = 5$
4. $3 + 2 = 5$
5. $5 + 1 = 6$
6. $1 + 2 = 3$
7. $2 + 2 = 4$

Page 11

1–3. Check drawings.
1. 4, 4
2. 6, 6
3. 5, 5
4. Circle first and middle cube trains.

Page 12

1–6. Check drawings.
1. 2
2. 3
3. 5
4. 1
5. 6
6. 4
7. Circle less than 5.

Page 13

1–3. Check drawings.
1. 3
2. 5
3. 6
4. Check drawing. 6 circles

Page 14

1–4. Order of responses will vary.
1. $1 + 2$
2. $2 + 1$
3. $0 + 3$
4. $3 + 0$
5–9. Order of responses will vary.
5. $1 + 3$
6. $3 + 1$
7. $0 + 4$
8. $4 + 0$
9. $2 + 2$
10. 7, 5; Circle 5.

Page 15

1–6. Order of responses will vary.
1. $2 + 3$
2. $3 + 2$
3. $1 + 4$
4. $4 + 1$
5. $0 + 5$
6. $5 + 0$
7–13. Order of responses will vary.
7. $2 + 4$
8. $4 + 2$
9. $1 + 5$
10. $5 + 1$
11. $0 + 6$
12. $6 + 0$
13. $3 + 3$
14. No

Page 16

1. $1 + 3 = 4$
2. $2 + 4 = 6$
3. $3 + 2 = 5$
4. more than 4¢

Page 17

1. $5 + 0 = 5$
2. $3 + 2 = 5$
3. $2 + 2 = 4$
4. $4 + 1 = 5$
5. Circle first and second groups.

Page 18

1. 3, 1; 2
2. 5, 1; 4
3. 2, 1; 1
4. 3, 1; 2

146

Page 19

1. $4 - 2 = 2$
2. $5 - 2 = 3$
3. $6 - 2 = 4$
4. $3 - 1 = 2$
5. $5 - 1 = 4$
6. $2 - 1 = 1$
7. 5, 3, 2
8. 6, 4, 2

Page 20

1. 2
2. 0
3. 0
4. 4
5. 5
6. 6
7. 0
8. 0
9. 2

Page 21

1. 2
2. 5
3. 3
4. 3
5. 4
6. 5
7. $6 - 3 = 3$

Page 22

1. Subtract
2. Add
3. $4 - 1 = 3$
4. $2 + 3 = 5$
5. $6 - 0 = 6$
6. $4 + 1 = 5$
7. $+, -, +$

Page 23

1–5. Order of responses will vary.
1. 2, 2
2. 4, 0
3. 0, 4
4. 1, 3
5. 3, 1
6. 2, 5, 0
7. 0, 1, 1
8. 1, 1, 2
9. 0, 3, 5
10. 3, 3, 0
11. less than 9

Page 24

1–6. Order of responses will vary.
1. 5, 0
2. 0, 5
3. 3, 2
4. 2, 3
5. 4, 1
6. 1, 4
7. 3, 4, 5
8. 3, 4, 5
9. 4, 3, 2
10. 4, 3, 2
11. Circle the first one.
    7, 8, 9

Page 25

1. 2
2. 4
3. 6
4. 1
5. 0
6. 5
7. 2
8. 1
9. Check drawings. 6 dots,
   1 dot

Page 26

1. 6, 5, 1
2. 6, 2, 4
3. 5, 2, 3
4. more than 4, less than 4,
   more than 3, less than 3

Page 27

1. How many are left?
2. How many in all?
3. How many in all?
4. How many are left?
5. How many are left?
6. How many in all?
7. $4 - 1 = 3$

Page 28

1. 5, 6
2. 9, 7
3. 6, 4
4. 7, 8, 9
5. 10, 9, 8
6. $10 + 2$

Page 29

1. 5, 7, 3, 10
2. 3, 6, 9, 2, 10, 8
3. 6, 10, 8, 4, 7, 9
4. 9, 8, 10, 10, 9, 8
5. 7, 6, 9, 10, 7, 6
6. $9 + 1$

Page 30

1. 7
2. 9
3. 9
4. 8
5. 7
6. 9
7. 10

Page 31

1. $6 + 3 = 9, 4 + 2 = 6,$
   $5 + 3 = 8$
2. $8 + 2 = 10, 5 + 2 = 7,$
   $3 + 3 = 6$
3. Answers will vary.

Page 32

1. Circle 9, 10; circle 6, 8; circle 3, 5;
   circle 4, 6; circle 4, 7; circle 7, 9
2. Circle 4, 5; circle 8, 10; circle 5, 8;
   circle 4, 5; circle 5, 6; circle 7, 10
3. Circle $1 + 8$; 9, 10
4. Circle $2 + 5$; 8, 7
5. Circle $4 + 2$; 7, 6

Page 33

1. 4, 8; 1, 2
2. 0, 0; 5, 10
3. 6, 2, 8, 4, 0, 10
4. 8; 8; circle $3 + 3$, 6; circle $0 + 0$, 0;
   9; circle $5 + 5$, 10
5. Circle $4 + 4$, 8; 10; 8; circle $2 + 2$,
   4; 7; circle $1 + 1$, 2
6. 7

Page 34

Check table:

Row 1: 2, 3, 6, 8
Row 2: 4, 5, 7
Row 3: 3, 9
Row 4: 4, 5, 6, 8
Row 5: 7, 10
Row 6: 6, 9
Row 7: 8, 10
Row 8: 8, 10
Row 9: 9

Peter and Jane

Page 35

1. $6 + 4 = 10$; $3 + 7 = 10$
2. $7 + 1 = 8$; $2 + 6 = 8$
3. 10, 8, 8, 10, 9, 7
4. 9, 10, 9, 10, 9, 10
5. Circle 1 and 4; $5 + 5 = 10$.

Page 36

1. $5 + 1 + 2 = 8$; 8
2. $3 + 3 + 3 = 9$; 9
3. $4 + 1 + 4 = 9$; 9
4. Answers will vary.

Page 37

1. $3 + 2 = 5$; 5
2. $5 + 2 = 7$; 7
3. $6 + 3 = 9$; 9
4. $4 + 3 = 7$; 7
5. Answers will vary.

Page 38

1. Draw a line through "There are 2 trucks on the road."; $4 + 3 = 7$; 7.
2. Draw a line through "He sees 1 train, too."; $4 + 4 = 8$; 8.
3. Draw a line through "Anna counts 5 trees."; $3 + 6 = 9$; 9.
4. Answers will vary.

Page 39

1. 3, 2, 4
2. 5, 3, 7
3. 4, 5, 2
4. 7, 1, 9
5. 6, 8, 8
6. 4
7. 6

Page 40

1. 7, 9, 3, 4, 2, 5
2. 1, 8, 3, 2, 7, 6
3. 6, 7, 8, 4, 4, 5
4. 2

Page 41

1. Check coloring: 2, 7, 6; 5, 7, 6; 4, 3, 5
2. 6, 2, 2, 4, 8, 4
3. Circle $7 - 3$; 6, 4
4. Circle $8 - 2$; 7, 6
5. Circle $9 - 3$; 7, 6

Page 42

1. 5
2. 3
3. 5
4. 6
5. 3
6. 6
7. Answers will vary.

Page 43

1. 5, 1, 3, 0, 5, 3
2. 7, 2, 3, 1, 7, 3
3. 8, 2, 5, 2, 6, 3
4. 4, 3, 2, 3, 9, 1
5. Circle child on far left.

Page 44

1. $5 + 1 = 6$; $6 - 1 = 5$
2. $7 + 2 = 9$; $9 - 2 = 7$
3. $6 + 3 = 9$; $9 - 3 = 6$
4. $4 + 4 = 8$; $8 - 4 = 4$
5. Add

Page 45

1. 6, 6, 5, 1; 5, 1, 6; 4, 4, 3, 1; 3, 1, 4; 5, 5, 2, 3; 2, 3, 5
2. 8, 8, 6, 5, 2; circle $7 - 2$.
3. 8, 8, 7, 3, 5; circle $4 + 3$.
4. 3, 2

Page 46

1–5. Check coloring and marking.
6. cube

Page 47

1. Circle first, third, and fourth shapes.
2. Draw an X on the first, middle, and last shapes.
3. Color first four shapes.
4. Circle the cone. No shapes can be stacked on the point of the cone.

Page 48

1. rectangle to rectangular prism, triangle to pyramid, circle to cylinder, square to cube
2. Circle last shape.

Page 49

1. 2
2. 6
3. 1
4. 6
5. 0
6. Circle the cylinder.

Page 50

1. Color square and circle. Circle middle two figures.
2. Color circle and triangle. Circle first and last figures.
3. Color first and third figures.
4. C, G, N, S

Page 51

1–6. Check coloring.
1. 3, 3
2. 4, 4
3. 8, 8
4. 5, 5
5. 3, 3
6. 4, 4
7. open figure

Page 52

1. Circle squares and triangles.
2. Circle square and rectangles.
3. Circle square and rectangles.
4. Circle the circles.
5. 3 corners or 3 sides

Page 53

1. Circle second figure.
2. Circle second figure.
3. Circle first figure.
4. Circle cone and cylinder.

Page 54

1. Circle first figure.
2. Circle first figure.
3. Circle second figure.
4. Check drawings.

Page 55

1. 6
2. 8
3. 10
4. cone, cylinder
5. cube, rectangular prism

Page 56

1–3. Check drawings.
1. 3
2. 2
3. 8

Page 57

1. Circle first and last.
2. Circle first and last.
3. Circle first and second.
4. Check drawing.

Page 58

1–4. Lines drawn may vary.
1. hexagon, trapezoid
2. rhombus, hexagon
3. triangle, rhombus
4. triangle, trapezoid
5. 2 triangles, 1 rhombus, 0 trapezoids, 0 hexagons

Page 59

1. 3, 30
2. 2, 20
3. 5, 50
4. 4 groups of 10

Page 60

1. 1, 10
2. 2, 20
3. 4, 40
4. 5, 50
5. 6, 60
6. 8, 80
7. 7 tens
8. 50

Page 61

1. 1, 1; 11
2. 1, 2; 12
3. 1, 6; 16
4. 2, 0; 20
5. fewer than 10

Page 62

1. 30
2. 50
3. 7
4. 40
5. 21

Page 63

1. 65, 36, 54
2. 36
3. 80
4. 54
5. 79
6. Circle first group.

Page 64

1. 74, 84, 94
2. 65
3. 29
4. 41
5. 98
6. 7 tens 6 ones

Page 65

Circle 1–4 in blue.
1. 55
2. 48
3. 82
4. 69
5. Circle in red 34; 12, 41, 29, 21, 22, 44, 20, 38.

Page 66

1. 15, 12; Circle 15.
2. 41, 49; Circle 49.
3. 4, 7; Circle 4.
4. 30, 8; Circle 8.
5. 20, 11; Circle 11.
6. 46, 52; Circle 46.
7. 75
8. 66

Page 67

1. >, <, >
2. >, >, <
3. <, <, <
4–5. Answers will vary.
6. a number that comes after 75

Page 68

1. 21, 23; 46, 48; 96, 98
2. 38, 13, 21; 92, 26, 79; 23, 87, 33; 62, 45, 81
3. Yes
4. Yes

Page 69

Table: 2, 3, 12, 13, 22, 23, 32, 33, 42, 43, 52, 53, 62, 63, 72, 73, 82, 83, 92, 93
1. Circle red: 3, 6, 9, 12, 15, 18, 21, 24, 27, 30.
2. Circle blue: 2, 4, 6, 8, 10, 12, 14, 16, 18, 20, 22, 24, 26, 28, 30.
3. 51, 61

Page 70

1. 12, 14, 17, 19
2. 21, 24, 26, 27, 29
3. 38, 40, 41, 42, 44, 46
4. 92, 93, 97, 98, 99
5. 51, 53, 55, 56, 57, 60
6. 84, 85

Page 71

1. 62, 63, 64, 66, 68, 69, 70
2. 58, 59, 60, 62, 63, 64, 65
3. 21, 22, 25, 26, 27, 28, 29
4. 47, 48, 49, 51, 52, 53
5. 33, 35, 36, 37, 40, 41
6. 90, 91, 93, 94, 96, 98
7. 15, 16, 17, 18, 19

Page 72

1. 41, 42, 43, 44, 45, 46, 47, 48
2. 56, 57, 58, 59, 60, 61, 62, 63
3. 38, 39, 40, 41, 42, 43, 44, 45
4. 103, 104, 105, 106, 107, 108, 109, 110
5. 97, 98, 99, 100, 101, 102, 103, 104
6. Draw six marbles: 112, 113, 114, 115, 116, 117.

149

Page 73

1. 11, 21, 31, 41, 51, 61, 71, 81, 91
2. 24, 34, 44, 54, 64, 74, 84, 94, 104
3. 17, 27, 37, 47, 57, 67, 77, 87, 97
4. 39, 49, 59, 69, 79, 89, 99, 109, 119
5. 15, 25, 35, 45, 55, 65, 75, 85, 95
6. 22, 32, 42, 52, 62, 72, 82, 92, 102
7. 36, 46, 56, 66, 76, 86, 96, 106, 116
8. 13, 23, 33, 43, 53, 63, 73, 83, 93
9. 18, 28, 38, 48, 58, 68, 78, 88, 98
10. 80

Page 74

1. 105
2. 102
3. 106
4. 101
5. 109
6. 104

Page 75

1. 114
2. 110
3. 119
4. 116
5. 118
6. 112
7. 120

Page 76

1. 62 = 62; Possible answer: 6 tens 2 ones and 5 tens 12 ones
2. 38 = 38; Possible answer: 3 tens 8 ones and 1 ten 28 ones
3. 47 = 47; Possible answer: 4 tens 7 ones and 2 tens 27 ones

Page 77

1. 3 + 4 = 7; 7 − 4 = 3
2. 6 + 2 = 8; 8 − 2 = 6
3. 4 + 6 = 10; 10 − 6 = 4
4. 5 + 5 = 10; 10 − 5 = 5
5. 6 + 3 = 9; 9 − 3 = 6
6. Possible Answer: 7 − 2 = 5

Page 78

1. Circle 6, 8; circle 6, 9; circle 7, 10; circle 8, 9; circle 7, 9; circle 9, 12.
2. Circle 9, 10; circle 9, 11; circle 8, 10; circle 5, 8; circle 8, 11; circle 5, 7.
3. Circle 6, 7; circle 7, 10; circle 7, 8; circle 9, 11; circle 9, 12; circle 6, 9.
4. 7

Page 79

1. Circle 3 + 3; 6, 8, 11
2. Circle 6 + 6 and 4 + 4; 6, 12, 8
3. Circle 2 + 2 and 5 + 5; 4, 10, 8
4. Circle 1 + 1 and 3 + 3; 2, 8, 10, 10, 6, 9
5. Circle 5 + 5, 4 + 4, and 6 + 6; 8, 10, 8, 9, 11, 12
6. 4 + 4 = 8

Page 80

1. 10, 11, 5, 2, 8, 3
2. 9, 6, 0, 7, 4, 1
3. 9
4. 1
5. 5
6. 3
7. 11
8. 7

Page 81

1. 10, 10, 10, 11, 9, 9
2. 6, 12, 8, 12, 11, 11
3. less than 10; more than 10

Page 82

1. 9, 10, 11, 12
2. 5, 6, 7, 8
3. 2 + 6 to 6 + 2; 3 + 7 to 7 + 3; 2 + 5 to 5 + 2
4. 0 + 8 to 8 + 0; 2 + 8 to 8 + 2; 3 + 6 to 6 + 3
5. 4
6. 5

Page 83

1. 9, 7, 6, 6, 5, 8
2. 9, 8, 9, 7, 4, 6
3. 8, 7, 5, 5, 9, 4
4. 50 − 1

Page 84

1. 1, 3, 2, 3
2. 2, 2, 1, 3
3. 1, 2, 1, 3, 2, 2
4. 4, 3, 1, 2, 3, 2
5. Check work: 3, 9, 3, 8, 7, 2

Page 85

1. 11, 6
2. 11, 7
3. 10, 5
4. 12, 8
5. 11, 9
6. 12, 6
7. 10, 7
8. 12, 7
9. Add

Page 86

1. 10, 10, 9, 3, 7; circle 6 + 3 = 9
2. 9, 9, 1, 7, 8; circle 8 − 1 = 7
3. 8, 9, 9, 2, 7; circle 2 + 6 = 8
4. 8, 8, 3, 4, 5; circle 9 − 5 = 4
5. 5

Page 87

1. 11; 5 + 6 = 11; 9 + 2 = 11
2. 10; 4 + 6 = 10; 2 + 8 = 10
3. Answers will vary. Possible answer: 3, 4, 6; 3 + 4 + 6 = 13; 7 + 6 = 13; 3 + 10 = 13

Page 88

1. Add; 9 + 3 = 12; 12
2. Subtract; 9 − 5 = 4; 4
3. Subtract; 11 − 3 = 8; 8
4. Check work.

Page 89

1. $5 + 5 = 10$
2. $8 - 6 = 2$
3. $11 - 2 = 9$
4. Answers will vary.

Page 90

1–6. Check drawings.
7. Circle bottom toothbrush.

Page 91

1. longer; Check drawings.
2. shorter; Check work.

Page 92

1–4. Answers will vary.
5. Circle second answer.

Page 93

1–4. Answers will vary.
5. Circle first picture.

Page 94

1. cube—8, cone—3, cylinder—5, rectangular prism—6
2. W

Page 95

1–4. Answers will vary.

Page 96

1. Check graph.
2. triangle
3. 16
4. Questions will vary.

Page 97

1. Questions will vary.
2. Questions will vary.

Page 98

1. 10
2. 13
3. 15
4. 20
5. Questions will vary.

Page 99

1. Circle second question.
2. Circle first question.
3. Questions will vary.
4. Questions will vary.

Page 100

1. Circle second banana.
2. Circle first watermelon.
3. Circle first plate.
4. Circle second plate.
5. Circle top bag.
6. Circle top loaf.
7. Check drawing.

Page 101

1–4. Check drawings.
5. Color half of second and third shapes.
6. 2

Page 102

1. $\frac{1}{3}, \frac{1}{4}, \frac{1}{2}$
2. $\frac{1}{4}, \frac{1}{2}, \frac{1}{3}$
3. Color $\frac{1}{4}$ of second and third shapes.
4. $\frac{1}{3}$

Page 103

1–9. Circle images 2, 3, 4, 7, 8, 9.
10. Circle second shape.

Page 104

1–6. Check coloring.
7. $\frac{1}{3}$

Page 105

Check calendar.
1–4. Answers depend on month.
5. Answer depends on months compared.

Page 106

1. 3
2. 7
3. 10
4. 8
5. 5
6. 9
7. 6

Page 107

1. Check drawings.
2. 6:00, 4:00, 2:00
3. 12:00

Page 108

1–3. Check work.
4. 6:00

Page 109

1–6. Check work.
7. 3:00

Page 110

1. 8:00, 12:30, 1:30
2. 2:30, 9:00, 5:00
3. Check work.
4. more than 30 minutes

Page 111

1. 9:30, 1:30, 11:00
2. 12:30, 5:00, 4:30
3. 6:00, 7:30, 11:30
4. 8:30

Page 112

1–3. Check drawings for 4:00, 12:30, 10:00.
4. Answers will vary.

Page 113

1–4. Check work.
5. Circle second picture.
6. Circle first picture.

Page 114

1. 3
2. 4
3. 2
4. 5
5. 4
6. 3
7. Circle second purse; draw an X on the first purse.

Page 115

1. 12
2. 35
3. 63
4. 44
5. Circle first group.

151

Answer Key
Core Skills Math, Grade 1

Page 116

1. Circle 2 dimes.
2. Circle 4 dimes.
3. Circle 6 dimes.
4. Circle 6 nickels.
5. Circle 5 dimes.
6. Circle 2 nickels.
7. 4 dimes

Page 117

1. 20
2. 8
3. 40
4. 25; circle the two dimes and the nickel
5. 25; circle nickels
6. 70
7. 25¢

Page 118

Circle 1, 5, 6, 9, 10, 12.
Cross out 2, 3, 4, 7, 8, 11.
13. Check work.

Page 119

1. 7, 7
2. 5, 5
3. 8, 8
4. 9, 9
5. 17, 17
6. 16, 16
7. 12

Page 120

1. 7, 7, 7
2. 5, 5, 5
3. 9, 9, 9
4. 9, 9, 9
5. Check drawing; trapezoid.

Page 121

1. −
2. +
3. −
4. +
5. −
6. −
7. +
8. +
9. 11
10. Answers will vary.

Page 122

1. 9
2. 6
3. 1
4. 4
5. 5
6. 3
7. 6
8. 2
9. 2
10. 7
11. 5
12. 16

Page 123

1–4. Check work.
1. 14
2. 26
3. 33
4. 18
5. more than 30
6. between 10 and 30

Page 124

1. 38, 58
2. 15, 35
3. 63, 83
4. 79, 99
5. 18, 28
6. 27, 37
7. 6

Page 125

1. $40 + 20 = 60$
2. $30 + 30 = 60$
3. $30 + 10 = 40$
4. $60 + 20 = 80$
5. $40 + 40 = 80$
6. $10 + 50 = 60$
7. $7 + 1$ to 8; $20 + 10$ to 30; $2 + 4$ to 6
8. $40 + 30$ to 70; $20 + 20$ to 40; $5 + 4$ to 9

Page 126

1–10. Answers will vary.
11. 37
12. 38

Page 127

1. 49
2. 76
3. 27
4. 44
5. 89
6. 37; Check explanation.

Page 128

1. 49
2. 86
3. 98
4. 59
5. 15
6. 77
7. 87
8. 45
9. 79
10. 89
11. 41; Check explanation.

Page 129

1–3. Check drawings.
1. 31
2. 72
3. 43
4. 36; Check work.

Page 130

1–2. Check drawings.
1. 5, 7; $50 + 7 = 57$; 57
2. 8, 8; $80 + 8 = 88$; 88
3. $36 + 22 = 58$; $22 + 36 = 58$

Page 131

1. 80, 70, 50, 40, 70
2. 60, 20, 90, 20, 90
3. 90, 90, 30, 30, 70
4. 53, 63, 73, 83, 93
5. 33, 43, 53, 63, 73

Page 132

1. 9; 5, 9; 6, 9
2. 10; 6, 10; 5, 10
3. Answers will vary.

Page 133

1. 2, 1; 4, 2; 6, 3
2. 8, 4; 10, 5; 12, 6
3. 14, 7; 16, 8; 18, 9

Answer Key
Core Skills Math, Grade 1

Page 134

1. 3
2. 9
3. 1
4. 16, 17
5. 14, 15
6. 10, 6, 13, 9, 4, 7
7. 5, 16, 11, 17, 8, 12
8. 11
9. 13

Page 135

1. 7
2. 13
3. 15
4. 17
5. 11
6. 18, 13, 7, 2, 17, 14
7. 16, 1, 9, 15, 8, 10
8. Check work.

Page 136

1. 11, 14, 12, 12, 14, 13
2. 15, 11, 12, 11, 13, 16
3. 14, 13, 16, 11, 11, 12
4. 1
5. 2

Page 137

1–3. Answers will vary.
4. 16, 15
5. 10, 11

Page 138

1. 5, 5, 7, 7, 9, 9
2. 8, 8, 16, 0, 8, 4
3. 12, 12, 10, 10, 12, 12
4. 7

Page 139

1. 6, 6
2. 7, 7
3. 4, 4
4. 9, 9
5. 8, 8
6. $18 - 9 = 9$ or $9 + 9 = 18$; 9

Page 140

1–4. Order of addends may vary.
1. 7; $7 + 5 = 12$;
   9, $9 + 5 = 14$; 4, $4 + 6 = 10$
2. 6, $6 + 3 = 9$;
   5, $5 + 8 = 13$; 7, $7 + 4 = 11$
3. 4, $4 + 8 = 12$;
   7, $7 + 7 = 14$; 7, $7 + 6 = 13$
4. 2, $2 + 9 = 11$;
   2, $2 + 6 = 8$; 6, $6 + 8 = 14$
5. 9
6. 6

Page 141

1. 12, 4; 16, 8; 13, 8
2. 17, 9; 15, 7; 11, 2
3. 14, 7; 15, 6; 18, 9
4. Make a 10.
5. Count on.
6. Add doubles.

Page 142

1–4. Order may vary.
1. $6 + 7 = 13$, $13 - 7 = 6$,
   $7 + 6 = 13$, $13 - 6 = 7$
2. $6 + 9 = 15$, $15 - 9 = 6$,
   $9 + 6 = 15$, $15 - 6 = 9$
3. $8 + 4 = 12$, $12 - 4 = 8$,
   $4 + 8 = 12$, $12 - 8 = 4$
4. $6 + 5 = 11$, $11 - 5 = 6$,
   $5 + 6 = 11$, $11 - 6 = 5$
5. fewer than 9, 7

Page 143

1. 5
2. 6
3. 2
4. 5
5. 4
6. 7
7. 3
8. 8
9. 9
10. 3
11. 6
12. 8
13. 9; Check work.

Page 144

1. Cross out, "Eddie has 6 sea plants."
   $12 - 5 = 7$; 7
2. Cross out, "There are 12 boats."
   $9 + 8 = 17$; 17
3. Cross out, "Today Marta found 4 crabs." $10 - 6 = 4$; 4
4. Possible answers:
   $4 + 5 = 9$, $5 + 4 = 9$,
   $9 - 5 = 4$, $9 - 4 = 5$,
   $5 - 4 = 1$

Page 145

1–8. Circled addends will vary.
1. 13
2. 10
3. 15
4. 10
5. 12
6. 13
7. 11
8. 16
9. $4 + 3 + 3 = 10$; Order of addends may vary. Check drawings.